The Skaneateles Religious Society
a.k.a.
The First Presbyterian Church of Skaneateles, NY

Rev. Dr. Craig Lindsey

David Russell Tulloch

Parson's Porch & Book Publishing Company

Turning words into books & Turning books into bread

The Skaneateles Religious Society a.k.a. The First Presbyterian Church of Skaneateles, NY

ISBN: Softcover

Copyright © 2017 by Craig Lindsey

All rights reserved. No part of this book may be reproduced or transmitted in any form or by any means, electronic or mechanical, including photocopying, recording, or by any information storage and retrieval system, without permission in writing from the publisher.

To order additional copies of this book, contact:

Parson's Porch Books
1-423-475-7308
www.parsonsporch.com

Parson's Porch Books is an imprint of **Parson's Porch & Book Publishers** in Cleveland, Tennessee, which has double focus. We focus on the needs of creative writers who need a professional publisher to get their work to market, **&** we also focus on the needs of others by sharing our profits with those who struggle in poverty to meet their basic needs of food, clothing, shelter and safety.

This material was researched, edited, and published in honor of the 215th Anniversary of The Congregation of The First Presbyterian Church in 2016 Coincident with the 125th Anniversary of the Sanctuary Constructed in 1891.

Contents

Preface 7
Origins of The Church, Community 11
And Religious Society
    THE SCHANEATELES RELIGIOUS SOCIETY 13
    THE CHURCH ARTICLES of 1801 15
    A CONFESSION OF FAITH 1801 16
    THE COVENANT OF 1801 17
    QUESTIONS OF PROFESSING CHRISTIANS 17
    ORGANIZING THE FIRST, FIRST PRESBYTERIAN CHURCH ... 18
    THE CHURCH'S BUILDINGS 20
    THE 1831 CHURCH BUILDING 21
    THE OLD CHURCH POEM 22
    THE FIRST PIPE ORGAN 24
    THE CURRENT SANCTUARY (1892) 27
    THE CHURCH BELL 29
    CHURCH PARKING 29
    THE STAINED-GLASS WINDOWS 29
    THE 1928 RENOVATIONS 56
    THE 1950'S ADDITIONS 57
    DOBSON HALL 58
    THE ACADEMY STREET MANSE 59
    THE ORGAN TASK FORCE 60
    THE LITURGICAL DESIGN TASK FORCE 60
    THE ALL CHURCH TASK FORCE 63
    RE-LEADING THE STAINED-GLASS WINDOWS 64
    THE RENOVATION STEERING GROUP 1994-1996 65
    CAPITAL FUND I 1995-2000 65
    RENOVATION STEERING GROUP II 1997-98 RSG II 66
    CAPITAL FUND II 67
    THE PURPOSE OF REBUILDING 68

CONSTRUCTION FINANCING	70
DOBSON HALL REBUILDING	72
THE CHURCH IN TRANSITION	73
THE CHURCH'S PASTORS	74
THE TRIALS AND TRIBULATIONS OF THE CHURCH	79
PROFESSORS OF RELIGION	79
THE TWO "FIRST PRESBYTERIAN" CHURCHES	81
MORE RECENT HISTORIC CONFLICTS	83
THE CO-PASTORATE	85
MEMBERSHIP STATISTICS	87
SPECIALIZED MINISTRIES	91
THE SABBATH SCHOOL	91
THE MINISTRY OF MUSIC	95
THE MARGARET SPITZER ENDOWMENT	97
THE CROSSMAN/SODERBERG SCHOLARSHIP	97
THE PRESBYTERIAN WOMEN'S ASSOCIATION AND CIRCLES	98
THE PRESBYTERIAN MEN	98
THE MINISTRY TO COMMUNITY YOUTH	98
THE DUK LOST BOYS' SUDANESE CLINIC and THE JOHN DAU FOUNDATION	99
THE CHURCH'S ENDOWMENTS	105
AN INVESTMENT MINISTRY	105
PRESBYTERIAN MANOR	106
A DIIFERENT WAY OF FUNDING MISSION	107
CONCLUSION	108

Preface

Earlier versions of this material were written 1896-2001, to provide the congregation a narrative history of God working upon, through and with the people of the First Presbyterian Church of Skaneateles. In the last fifteen years, significant systemic and infrastructure changes have been accomplished, and before first-hand experience is forever forgotten in history, we again pause to record, reflect and pray in Sabbath, that the church might have a spiritual witness of continuity for understanding, insight and planning. The difficulty of any history is the incorporation of cross-cultural interpretations and conflicting accounts of circumstances within that history. This account is based on:

- The Articles of Incorporation of the Schaneateles Religious Society
- The Minutes of the First Presbyterian Church of Skaneateles
- The Transcripts of Disciplinary Trials of the First Presbyterian Church
- The Sermons of Pastors of this Congregation
- Newspaper Articles of the time
- The histories written at earlier times in the life of this community of faith
- The first-hand Accounts and Records of the Pastor 1996-Present.

Every effort has been made to portray the most accurate and truthful of accounts; however, where earlier records may have been inaccurate, these discrepancies are noted, as the inaccuracies had become part of the accepted heritage known and shaping this community.

Often when histories are written, the narrative is a triumphal account recalling joys of accomplishment, and neglectful of the conflicts causing decision-making. The purpose of this tome, is to mark the way for this body, as well as for others who may witness and pass similar forks in the road in future generations, to learn from our mistakes, and without the corrected stigmatism of history to see the connection and transpiring of events.

When sailing, and forward is directly into the wind (*nephish*/spirit) a sailor tacks back and forth across the wind, using a centerboard, dagger or keel to prevent the craft from being blown over or from sliding backward. In Hebrew, there is a method of storytelling described as *seriatim* meaning little side-journeys along the way, which tell a fuller story of the truth. In sacred dance, the faithful take three steps forward and one step back, in this way making progress, but always rebalancing and centering.

As Western Society began a third millennium (2001), this congregation was privileged to begin our third century (founded in 1801). From a virgin wilderness, to rustic family farms cultivated by oxen and plow, to the building of the first dam raising the water-level of the lake, to the planting and harvesting of teasels, and the invention of the steamboat, to the populating of residences, industry and tourism in Skaneateles today, a continuing force of growth, development and cultural identity of this community has been The First Presbyterian Church. It has been said that those who do not learn the lessons of history are destined to repeat them. Our Christian identity, as well as our relationships and traditions, patterns and systems of behavior, all arise from our church's history.

In the Centennial celebration of this congregation (1801-1901) our heritage was lifted up by Rev. White. Noted were our Puritan ancestry, having descended from those who landed on Plymouth Rock, the hard work and ministry done throughout Skaneateles, the respect enjoyed by this community, and our beautiful church building. Rev. O.L. White, installed pastor at the time, affirmed:

> "This has not by any means been an ideal church, the perfect church is in heaven. Another history may have been written, whose tone would be adversely critical, in which the facts stated would be justifiably censurable because of folly or maliciousness. But every historian or biographer omits more than he records, and wisely. Among the early settlers were men of military title, and they carried their belligerent propensities into church matters as well. Considering the number of such experiences, it is a wonder that the church ever survived. Bitter feelings engendered, and autocratic inquisitorial exercise of power, resulted in several divisions within this body. It is no small thing, to have been an organization, in which a thousand souls have confessed their faith in Christ, and acknowledged his mastery, while half as many more having come from other churches have cast their lot in and found a religious home. We believe in God; we believe in His purpose for us in the future, and therefore we have abundant courage. We begin the second century under auspicious skies. Undoubtedly there will be dark periods; there have been many in the century past; hardships and sacrifices, doubtless will be required – they have been before – but with a mighty God, with faithful, loyal members, with

a universal gospel invitation to proclaim, with daily grace from the God of all graces, and the covenant that as our days our strength shall be, we resolutely face the future, actuated by Christian faith, hope and courage."

Origins of The Church, Community And Religious Society

When this church was founded in 1801, Europe was in the turmoil of war between France and Austria, then all Europe, as Napoleon Bonaparte led his army over the Alps and 3 years later was crowned Emperor of France and Italy. On our own soil, Thomas Jefferson had been elected President of the United States and Robert Fulton had invented the Steam driven engine. Our new Nation was in its infancy, everything west of the Hudson River, from Central New York to California was unexplored frontier.

The north end of Skaneateles Lake had been a meeting ground for the Iroquois tribes of the Onondaga and Cayugas. The outlet had not yet been dammed, and the water level was eight feet lower than at present. While forests of virgin timber reached to the water's edge, the hills surrounding the lake were blanketed in the texture of hardwoods. Along what today is Genesee Street was a dense forest of ash and hemlock trees. The town of Oswego was the nearest settlement.

While St. James' Episcopal Church claims Moravian Missionaries prayed on the Northshore of Skaneateles lake prior to the War for Independence in 1750, according to Clark's <u>History of Onondaga</u> (the accepted authority on historic development) "the first white explorer" to this area was John Thompson in 1793. Leslie's <u>History of Skaneateles</u> grants the title of "first settler" to Abraham Cuddeback. Cuddeback is described having come here from Orange County, New York. He left there October 2, 1793 with one wagon, three yoked pair of oxen, a two-year-old colt, a dozen milk cows, his wife and eighteen children, traveling from Albany by way of Fort Schuyler, today called Utica. Cuddeback arrived at the southern tip of the lake on June 14, 1794 having spent forty-three days of the road; whereupon he fashioned a raft and conveyed all his family and their effects downstream to the north shore.

Discovery of a large coned thistle-like plant called the "teasel", indigenous to this area, brought farming and industrial development to Skaneateles. The natural prickly spines of the teasel were found useful in separating the fibers of raw wool for the textile industry. Once harvested and cleaned, the brittle teasels were mounted to a drum that rolled over wool separating fibers, releasing dirt and debris for the carding and spinning of thread and yarn.

As their pilgrim forefathers had come to the New World to worship God freely in the 17th Century, the settlers of a hundred years later had a passion for Protestant religious belief and practices. The missionary movement of the 18th and 19th Centuries resulted in the establishment of many "congregational religious societies," which subsequently became Presbyterian. The congregations of Skaneateles, Marcellus and Elbridge all were formed in this era, Skaneateles being the first among these. Only eight years after the first explorer came to this region, seven years after the first settler arrived on a raft because there were no roads, the church began Christ's missionary enterprise.

Origin of the First Presbyterian Church in Skaneateles was as the Religious Society, without any denominational affiliation. The history of St. James' Episcopal Church claims that the Episcopalians wanted to worship separately from the rest of the Skaneateles Religious Society and were not granted a suitable time for worship in the community building, so founded a separate congregation in 1816 and erected their own church building in 1828. During different eras, relations between Christians have had our ebb and flow. In 2016, we are blessed with partnership and trust between the pastors and church members. However, there are distinctions between denominations which are preserved in there being different churches for important ecclesiastical reason. The Protestant Reformation had several stages. Martin Luther lived and died fighting for correction of errors and heresies within the one true church, as he was ordained a Catholic Priest, although excommunicated by that Church for his 95 Theses of 1517. The Evangelical Lutheran Church was created by those taking the writings of Martin Luther and codifying these in theology and practice. The Dutch Reformed Church and Presbyterian Church (USA) also derive from this Evangelical Lutheran branch of the Reformation. A different schism occurred from the Roman Catholic Church because King Henry VIII wished to be divorced (1534), and when the Roman Catholic Church excommunicated the King of England, he formed his own Church of England, identical in structure and liturgy, except that the Monarch of England is the Head of the Church in opposition to the Catholic Pope. One of the final decrees of Pope Benedict XVI (2013) was to declare that the Lutheran Reformation had ended, recognizing that changes within the Catholic Church, the Lutheran Church and its derivatives, were again one in Baptism. One of the vital differences for the Presbyterian Church from other denominations is that in the Presbyterian Church we only invest decision making authority in representative committees of the church, not in individuals like Priests, Bishops, Cardinals and the Pope. This means that while we minister together, pray and work together, we have a theological unity with the Roman Catholic, Lutheran and Reformed Churches; which we do not have with the Episcopal, Methodist, Baptist or Pentecostal Churches.

THE SCHANEATELES RELIGIOUS SOCIETY

The earliest worship services in this area were prayer meetings, conducted by itinerant missionaries from Connecticut sent out into this frontier from the General Association of Congregational Ministers, including the Revs.Seth Williston, David Higgins, Aaron Bascom, John Ingersoll and Caleb Alexander. These missionaries each nurtured the faith of the community for a few months, then moved on to be replaced several months later. The very first missionary to the area was the Rev. Mr. Osgood, and the first recorded preacher was the Rev. Thomas Robbins. The first evangelistic service on record, was held in a house in more recent times recorded as the home of E. Reuel and Sedgwick Smith, however at the time of the evangelistic service the home of David Seymour. The first incorporated local government for this area was in Marcellus, covering all of what is now Marcellus, Skaneateles and Skaneateles Falls, so one of the early identifications of these congregations meeting jointly is as The First Congregational Church of Marcellus.

On the 20th day of July, in the year of our Lord 1801, the Schaneateles congregation was organized by the Rev. Aaron Bascom of the New Hampshire Missionary Alliance with 15 members. The incorporators were Joshua Cook, Solomon Edwards, Simeon Hosmer, Asa Harwood, Daniel Cook, and Aaron Cook. On the 13th day of October 1801 Rev. Caleb Alexander organized a congregation at Marcellus with 18 members, meeting in the Tavern of Deacon Rice. Three months and nine days after the organizing of the Schaneateles congregation, on 29 October 1801 the Village of Marcellus records a meeting was held at the Marcellus Schoolhouse, for the purpose of establishing the Religious Society of Schaneateles, as agreeable to the law in such cases. Ebenezer Hawley and Aaron Cook were unanimously chosen as Superintendents of the Schaneateles Society.

Caleb Alexander
First Principal of Onondaga Academy

"Now we, the said Ebenezer Hawley and Aaron Cook, do hereby certify that the said Schaneateles Society did elect and chuse Ebenezer Hawley, Joseph Clift, Judah Hopkins, and Daniel Cook to be Trustees for said Society, and that the said Society should forever after be known and distinguished by the name The Schaneateles Religious Society."

There were fifteen original members of The Schaneateles Religious Society, seven men and eight women in 1801. The designation of being The Schaneateles Religious Society continues as the corporate name of the church through the present time. The last survivor of the original members was Mrs. Anna (Cook) Clark, who died 20 January 1860. Over the years, it has seemed odd to many, that Marcellus, Skaneateles, Skaneateles Falls, Elbridge, Weedsport, all were identified as being Marcellus; and yet the many different churches established in each of these towns were all titled The Schaneateles Religious Society… Only in recent years have we come to understand that in the early 19th Century the only Governmental offices were located in Marcellus, so legally these differing towns were all in Marcellus. However, "spiritually" this region had been named by the Native Onondagan peoples as "Schaneateles" along with the name of the main body of water. So when churches were named, they used the name Skaneateles.

However, in 1816, several members of the Skaneateles Religious Society (in Skaneateles) left the fellowship, preferring the Church of England style of worship and prayer. These formed what is today St. James Episcopal Church. The Skaneateles Religious Society continued, in 1818 formally being renamed The First Presbyterian Church of Skaneateles.

From 1820-1852 Roman Catholics met in one another's homes until building St. Mary's of the Lake Church.

In 1831, the Presbyterians sold the white clapboard church to the Baptists who continued to worship there until 1841 when they dismantled the structure rebuilding on County Route #321, which in the summer of 2016 received fresh siding. In 1831, realizing that the Village had developed here around the North-end of the Lake, and that it was difficult to climb the hill, especially by horse and wagon in the winter, the First Presbyterian Church built the second First Presbyterian building, this time on Genesee Street. There is no competition between the churches in the Village, if anything we partner and attempt to outdo one another in mission, service, ministry and celebrations. Following the paradigm of the 3 Little Pigs, where the first Church was built of wood, the second was built of brick! Except, there was little attention at the time of construction to the flow of the Lake from South to North, and over the next 60 years, the basement timbers rotted, as mortar was washed out from between bricks. During a Religious Revival in 1891, the balcony and floor began moving, so everyone was evacuated and the building was demolished into its own foundation. The 3rd Sanctuary was built that year, with the bulk of the cost paid by Mr. Thomas Hall, who had two conditions. The first was that "there would be a pew designated as a welcome place for strangers." Second, that his gift was to be used for structure, not artwork; so Rev. O.L. White contacted all of the original families of the Skaneateles Religious Society asking if they would like to be memorialized in the windows. While many had become part of other denominations, or lived elsewhere now, they contributed to the Stained-Glass windows making this an extremely ecumenical house of worship. When opened, the Sanctuary ceiling was orange with gold bands, the walls were Salmon pink, with red oak wainscoting, and a green asbestos tile flooring.

For many years, this Sanctuary was used for High School Commencement exercises, before development of the Gazebo in the park. Throughout the 1960s, dances were held for Youth from across the community with music by local bands. Beginning in 1995, the First Presbyterian Church building went through many renovations and updates, including re-leading the Windows, replacing the Pipe Organ, Nurseries and Community rooms, and installing air conditioning. In 1975 the church spun off Presbyterian Manor Suites as an independent affordable communal residence for Senior Citizens, located in the community. In 2001 First Presbyterian Church became the indoor venue for Skaneateles Festival concerts. That same year, the congregation sponsored refugees from South Sudan, which developed into the John Dau Foundation, providing health care to over 190,000 patients in a location that previously did not have running water or electricity. As part of this 215th Anniversary Sunday worship service three infants were baptized, representing the Skiff/ Brennan, Way/Clark , and Allyn /Earhart families; a hymn was sung, the lyrics of which were written by Mary Soderberg; Dr. Lindsey's sermon was on "Importunities as Important Opportunities."

THE CHURCH ARTICLES of 1801

1. We the undersigned profess to believe the Scriptures to be the only rule of faith and practice.
2. Every particular church hath a right to hear and determine all matters of disruption that respect its own members and that no Councils hath any right to determine for them or do anything binding on them without their consent.
3. As in the multitude of counsellors there is safety, it is advisable and allowed of by the gospel for a church as circumstances may be to call on members of other churches and be advised by them and that every Christian church ought to give account of its proceedings to other Christian churches when occasion calls for it.
4. A visible Christian church must consist of visible Christians, that is such as to appearance are true believers; for if they are not to appearance true believers, they cannot be proper objects of

brotherly love.

5. The infants or children of such as are members in full communion, and none other, are the proper objects of baptism.

A CONFESSION OF FAITH 1801

1) In general, we believe the articles of the Christian faith as they are contained in the Old and New Testaments. Particularly, we believe there is one only, living, true God, in three persons, the Father, the Son and the Holy Ghost, the Great Creator, Preserver and governor of all worlds and things.

2) We believe God made man in his own image, consisting in knowledge, righteousness and holiness, but that man by his disobedience has fallen from that holy and happy state and plunged himself into a state of sin and misery, out of which state he cannot recover himself, and in which he might justly have been left forever.

3) We believe that God, out of his mere goodness has opened a new way of life, by the mediation of Jesus Christ and all are invited to believe and trust in Christ and return to God through Him, and that there is no salvation in any other.

4) We believe that all to whom the Gospel comes, and it is their present indispensable duty, as well as for their interest, to return to God through Christ and embrace the Gospel, but that mankind are naturally so attached to sin as that there is not the least degree of ground to expect that anyone ever will of himself accept the Gospel salvation; but full reason to believe that all will go down to destruction unless prevented by the special, sovereign, forfeited grace of God.

5) We believe it pleases God in his own time and way, by the powerful application of the Holy Spirit, effectually to call and draw to Jesus Christ, all such as are ordained to eternal life; and that this effectual call is wholly of God's free and special grace alone.

6) We believe that all those who truly receive Jesus Christ, and are accepted of God through him, will persevere to the end of life, and finally be recovered by the grace of God, to a state of perfect holiness, being kept by the power of God through faith unto salvation.

7) And lastly, we believe that God hath appointed a day in which he will judge the world in righteousness by Jesus Christ, and that all true believers shall be received into the everlasting joy of their LORD, while all others shall be rejected and sent into everlasting punishment.

THE COVENANT OF 1801

We do now in the awful presence of the dread Majesty of Heaven and Earth, and before angels and men, with true seriousness and sincerity of soul, avouch the Lord Jehovah to be our Sovereign Lord and Supreme Good through Jesus Christ; and we solemnly devote and give up ourselves to his fear and service, engaging ourselves to observe all God's commandments, to seek his glory, and to walk in Christian fellowship, and a conscientious performance of all Christian duties, in all the ordinances of Christ, to be enjoyed in his church, and in this particular church, so long as God in his Providence shall continue us here, always depending on Jesus Christ to be enabled and assisted in the performance of these solemn vows.

Joshua Cook Solomon Edwards Simeon Hosmer
Asa Harwood Amiel Cook Aaron Cook: Incorporators

Three of the original fifteen members of the Schaneateles Religious Society were members of the Solomon Edwards family. The first funeral held by the Society was for Simeon Edwards. The first Wedding was a double ceremony for two daughters of the Edwards family. The first Baptism was for Simeon's grandson Ahsah, child of Alanson and Elizabeth Edwards. The heads of the Edwards family held office as Elders and Deacons of this church providing virtually continuous leadership from 1801 until 1936.

QUESTIONS OF PROFESSING CHRISTIANS

The following questions were earnestly recommended to the frequent and prayerful perusal of each member. These formed the outline for exhortation prior to receiving the Lord's Supper. These questions were then referred to again at the Centennial Anniversary of the church in 1901 as an Every Member Visitation.

1. Are you in practice of daily secret prayer?
2. Do you, who are heads of families, daily and regularly maintain the worship of God in your families?
3. Do you study the Scriptures daily?
Do you make it a matter of conscience to attend all the regular meetings for social worship, appointed by the church, unless providentially detained?
4. Do you labor and pray for the salvation of the unconverted around you?
5. Do you give conscientiously and systematically to the various objects of benevolence, as God has given you ability?

6. Do you regularly pray that God will bless his truth to the conviction and conversion of men?

7. Are you doing what you can to promote the Kingdom of Christ on Earth?

8. Do you pray daily for your minister and the members of the church?

9. Do you feel it your duty to consecrate all you have and are to the service of the Lord?

10. Will you remember to read these questions prayerfully, at least on each communion Sabbath?

The Lord's Supper, at that time, was administered on the first Sabbath in February, April, June, August, October and December. In 1997, the Session acted to celebrate the Lord's Supper regularly on the first Sunday of each month, or when it is theologically more appropriate to share together in communion. In 2001, the Session added that the Sacrament of the Lord's Supper also be celebrated regularly throughout the season of Lent, on Easter morning and Christmas Eve.

ORGANIZING THE FIRST, FIRST PRESBYTERIAN CHURCH

In those early days, it was not easy to secure anything like regularity in preaching. Itinerant Missionaries would preach a Sunday or two, then move on to another station. Instead, the Schaneateles Religious Society was originally established to ensure provision of three missions to the community. The Religious Society was called "to educate, adjudicate and exhort the people to faith." Before the creation of "public schools," the Religious Society taught the skills of reading, writing and arithmetic to adults and children using the Bible as a Primer. Also, before the institution of civil and criminal courts and justices, the Religious Society provided the adjudication of conflicts, hearing and resolving differences of opinion, disruptions of the peace, and other disturbances of the community. In an age when believers were required to have confessed their sins prior to receiving the Sacraments, the Trustees of the Religious Society were charged with listening to each of the members' confession prior to receiving the Lord's Supper, Marriage, Baptism of Children, or Burial. Tragically, this also led to the "autocratic, inquisitorial abuse of power" mentioned earlier, as the Trustees also represented the Heads of the principal families in the community.

After the organization of the church, the first preaching was by Rev. Mr. Thomas Robbins, a home missionary residing at the time at Marcellus. He came to Schaneateles now and then and preached in the local school house.

After Mr. Robbins, a Mr. Litherland from England, an uneducated man preached in the same place. When the young congregation outgrew the schoolhouse, they removed to a barn nearby, which offered more commodious quarters (there was also a log cabin used as a community gathering place, on what recently have been the grounds of Stella Maris Roman Catholic Retreat Center). When this proved unsatisfactory, the believers met in a local tavern operated by John Briggs, eventually becoming the site of what is today Shotwell Park. Divine Services were also held in the ballroom of the "Red House," currently painted green, built in 1798 at Willow Glen on the corner of Old Seneca and Jordan.

Great excitement prevailed among the early settlers when the dam, which had been built across the outlet near where the Stone Mill now stands, broke away. This circumstance occurred during a Saturday night and Sunday morning the people were all in consternation, for the breaking of the dam deprived the people of the facilities of their grist mill. The missionary, supposed to have been Rev. Isaac Rawson, preaching at the schoolhouse, learning of the catastrophe did not go to the place of meeting for worship that Sabbath morning. He sent a boy, directing him to tell the assembled congregation to adjourn and to assist in repairing the dam, as it was more important for them to have bread than to hear him preach. So, all that day, minister and people toiled, repairing the dam, which was thoroughly restored by nightfall.

In 1803, two years after their organization, the congregation voted to enter and become part of The Congregational Association, whose territorial boundaries covered this part of the State of New York. The young congregation seems to have engaged almost any kind of preacher that came along, and in consequence soon began to have trouble. Matters eventually became so distressing that the Congregational Association had to take affairs into hand and to Administer Censure against the members of the Religious Society. This admonition was graciously received, and in public meeting, the members voted that their differences should be healed and their ways mended.

However, yet another two years after this, on Christmas Day 25 December 1805, four years after incorporation, the membership of the Schaneateles Religious Society were called together for the resolution of a serious conflict, considered so severe as to be tearing apart the very fabric of Society. The conflict presented was whether the Schaneateles Religious Society should become a church or not. To be a church was described as requiring the building of a church building, rather than meeting in members' homes and community buildings. To be a church would require the calling and installing of a trained pastor to shepherd the flock, rather than sporadically hosting itinerant missionaries who enflamed the faith and outrage of believers. To be a church would require adopting specific programs of prayer meetings, worship and Bible Study for the whole of the community, rather than the four Trustees providing public education, judging disputes, and listening to the confessions of believers. By a recorded vote that Christmas Day of eight to seven, the Schaneateles Religious Society acted to become a church.

Association as a Presbyterian Church came in 1818, when by a vote of 18 to 15, the body united with the Presbytery of Cayuga as The First Presbyterian Church of Skaneateles. This relation continued until 1869, when by act of the General Assembly, the boundary lines of the Presbyteries were redefined and this church was placed within the Presbytery of Syracuse. In 1956, the Presbytery of Cayuga and the Presbytery of Syracuse merged to become the Presbytery of Cayuga-Syracuse, that very vote taking place at a Presbytery meeting in the Sanctuary of the First Presbyterian Church of Skaneateles.

THE CHURCH'S BUILDINGS

Planning for the new church building began immediately in 1806. An architect from Utica, NY was consulted and plans were drawn for the first church building. The congregation was as yet without a regular pastor, but by 1808 funds had been raised to such an extent as to justify beginning. The site chosen was the lot east of the school house atop the hill (the northern side of Onondaga Street, identified today as the intersection of Onondaga and Elizabeth streets). In so doing, the congregation followed the New England tradition of placing the House of God on the Point of Land nearest Heaven, to serve as a moral beacon, a light set on a hill, however inconvenient it may be for worshippers to climb that hill with supplies. Massive timbers in great abundance were used in the structure and the "raising" was a stupendous work. Construction of the building took six days. The community was divided into six districts, the men from each respective district coming for one day's work. The building was dedicated by The Rev. David Higgins on the first day of March, 1809. Total cost was $6,500 – a very large sum for those days, and especially so to be raised in a community only fifteen years old, containing roughly a hundred buildings, homes and barns.

The nearest completed church building was at Homer, erected in 1805. Auburn had no completed church until 1816, and the first churches in Rochester and Syracuse were not completed until 1826. The Marcellus Presbyterian Church which had begun as part of the same congregation, under the name The First Congregational Church of Marcellus began construction of their building prior to March 1809, but were unable to complete the structure until 1815. With the separation of the congregation into two locations and the Skaneateles Church completed first, the Skaneateles First Presbyterian Church was recognized by the denomination as being the successive body to the Schaneateles Religious Society established 20 July 1801.

THE 1831 CHURCH BUILDING

Less than twenty-two years later, a new church building was planned, having determined that the first site was in fact too far up the hill and too far outside the development of the incorporated village. The present site on Genesee Street was purchased from Mr. Spencer Parsons for $800 and the new church building made of brick, in similar design though larger was built for $6,000. The original church building was sold to the Baptist Society in 1831 and used for some time, then in 1841 dismantled, moved and rebuilt, at its present site on State Street, where the structure was improved and remains in use as a place of worship by that independent body.

The second church building, was built in 1831 during the pastorate of Rev. Brace, and was in use for sixty years. However, in December 1890, in the era of the Second Great Awakening (Jonathan Edwards and the Burned Over District), during the large attendance of an evangelistic worship service, led by Evangelist E.E. Davidson, the floor timbers and balcony began to move with settling. Temporary repairs averted what could have been a horrible tragedy that day.

Had the timbers settled further, support posts for the gallery would have collapsed, bringing down the roof and walls upon the praying congregation. Such extensive repairs were necessary to make the structure safe, that it was decided a new building was preferable. The 1831 masonry building was emptied, then collapsed into its foundations, for the construction of the new Sanctuary atop the stone firmament of the old church.

THE OLD CHURCH POEM

The following poem, written by Joyce Edwards was printed in The Advertiser Newspaper at the time the 1831 Presbyterian Church (Second) building was being demolished. While describing nothing specific to our own church, it conveyed the sentiments of many persons.

> Take them out tenderly, lift them with care,
> for every old timber is seasoned with prayer.
>
> Gently remove them – the old plastered walls,
> where sadly and faintly the last echo falls.

Take out the windows, the light streaming through,
though not dim, religiously lit every pew.

Where fathers and mothers united in prayer,
and we felt the spirit of worship was there.

There the youth and the maiden together hath stood,
plighting their troth in the presence of God,

There parents have promised to tenderly rear,
their children in holiness, justice and fear.

While out from the pulpit, so old and so worn,
dark warnings and threatenings often have come.

And gently God's promises fell on my ear,
to whisper of mercy dispelling each fear.

And hushed in the organ, its last solemn bay,
in darkness and silence is dying away

And tolling so mournfully sad, like a knell,
tolls the deep morning tones of the old worn out bell.

And silent the voices that once filled the choir,
they sang with spirit, and theirs the true fire.

But some have gone home – still praising God,
while others yet meekly pass under the rod.

Thy days are all numbered, old church on the green,
the last of thy stately pews soon will be seen.

Old things must go to make way for the new,
the hearts that once loved thee be scattered and few.

Then take down the pillars and unhinge the doors,
for one of the lessons that here we were taught,
was that the best work of man only cometh to naught.

Good-bye then, dear church, with windows so tall,
thy very plain aisles, thy old battered walls.

> We loved the old gallery, empty and cold,
> now frescoed all over with cobwebs and mold.
>
> But much we love thee, old church on the green,
> thou art growing too old, it is plain to be seen,
>
> And times busy fingers have done their work well,
> from pulpit to porch, from aisles to the bell.
>
> While time has been spoiling our church on the green,
> crowds of true worshippers weekly were seen;
>
> while the record is kept, for God's angels of love hath written it
> down in the temple above.

Throughout the 1890s demolition and construction, the congregation met for worship in the Village Library. Though there had been grave concerns about membership loss when there was no Sanctuary, actually the congregation grew in attendance.

THE FIRST PIPE ORGAN

A Johnson "Tracker-style" pipe organ was used in the 1831 church building, and reinstalled in the new 1892 church, with the console mounted on a platform identical to the Pulpit Dias against the North Chancel wall, the console located in the Northwest corner of the Sanctuary.

The Johnson Organ had originally been purchased for $1800 in 1879. In 1928, having already been moved 22 years after original installation, the Johnson Organ was donated to the Baptist Society for their worship, as the Johnson Organ was to be replaced by a Moeller Pipe Organ donated by Miss Anna Allen in memory of her brothers. The cost of removal of the Johnson Organ and re-installation at the Baptist church was completely paid for by Mr. F.E. Stone, a local attorney, and a Presbyterian who had sung in the Presbyterian Church Choir for many years. The Johnson Organ had ornamentally painted pipes, and the instrument continues in use today.

The 1891 Sanctuary with the original Johnson Tracker Pipe Organ, now at Baptist Church.

The 1927 Moeller Pipe Organ.

Tragically, in the late 1970s, when the Moeller Organ needed periodic re-leathering, the church leadership sought the cheapest remedy. Rather than professionally re-manufacturing problems with the organ by the manufacturer, the Session contracted with an individual who represented himself as an organ re-builder and did not check references. The rebuilt organ of 1979 looked far more contemporary, however re-leathering never occurred causing the organ to have a background sound like running water from escaping wind, also because he had carved off leather shallots with a box-cutter, the instrument was damaged beyond repair. Once the instrument had been changed, a master carpenter in the church membership crafted a beautiful case for it.

In 1998, The Organ Task Force, after a decade long search recommended replacement of the re-built Moeller with a new 40 Rank Casavant Organ. The Organ Task Force actually considered several alternatives. The Task Force rejected the idea of any electronic organ, on the basis that while greatly improved, these still synthesized the recorded sound of a pipe organ, and the committee preferred a true musical tone. Also, while the original cost of an electronic instrument is probably $1/10^{th}$ that of commissioning a new pipe organ, the life expectancy of an electronic organ is about 10 years, whereas pipe organs (if maintained) could last indefinitely. Controversy arose between those on the Organ Task Force who wanted to purchase a used instrument to be rebuilt versus those who wanted the church to commission a new instrument. While the cost was substantially greater, the congregation was swayed to commit to the commissioning of a new organ by the testimony of Bunt Osborne. Mr. Osborne had served as the church's organist for 40 years, having assumed the bench when his aunt had a heart-attack, she having begun as organist in 1923. "Bunt" described that "If the church wanted a rebuilt instrument, we already had one. But a new organ would be created as a work of art and craftsmanship for this space and our musical repertoire." The Casavant Organ was installed in 2003.

The 2003 Casavant Pipe Organ.

THE CURRENT SANCTUARY (1892)

The 1892 structure was completed at a cost of $30,000 fully five times the cost of the previous structure. The committee in charge of construction were the Trustees: Newell Turner, Emerson H. Adams, Thomas Kelley, R.V. Stackus, Philip Allen, John Parish, along with the Treasurer, S.L. Benedict. The architect was William Makepeace, and the builder was J.L. Schultz. The completed Sanctuary was dedicated 27 July 1892 during the pastorate of Rev. O.L. White. Mr. Thomas Hall of New York, NY had grown up in Skaneateles attending Sunday School here with his mother.

Mr. Hall gave generously toward the building program and its maintenance, in memory of his mother.

Mr. Hall's only specifications were that: he wanted to give to the glory of God, neither to music nor artwork (therefore wainscoting is considered structural), and that one pew shall be designated as "Reserved for strangers among us."

THE CHURCH BELL

The bell in the Southwest tower of the current church (1892) was originally given in 1848 for the second church, by five women teachers, Mrs. F. G. Jewett, Mrs. Charles Pardee, Mrs. Daniel Kellogg, Mrs. George F. Leitch, and Miss Chloe Hyde. Given records of the time, the actual first names of most of these women are unknown. The cost of the bell was $300.

CHURCH PARKING

Behind the church (to the North) in those days, were stables, for the sheltering of one's horse and carriage during worship, to keep them out of the snow or sun depending upon the season. What is today the Kitchenette off of the Sims Gathering Space, had previously been the Stable entrance to the church. On the east side of the church Sanctuary, the Narthex has a one meter drop, as this door had been the Funeral Casket exit, to take the casket from the Sanctuary to a waiting flatbed wagon. In 2013 this east entrance was converted to a Narthex restroom.

Years later, the church owned The Bond House (immediately to the west of the Sanctuary in this photo), and demolished that house to create the Church Parking lot.

THE STAINED-GLASS WINDOWS

All of the stained-glass windows in the Sanctuary were given as memorials. The 1892 church was nearing completion, and while Mr. Hall and members of the congregation had been extremely generous, contributing to the building of the facility while contributing to the Operating Budget, nothing had been set aside for the cost of the windows. The pastor set about contacting all of the families of the original Religious Society, suggesting that their heritage be immortalized in the windows. Therefore, the windows which shine light into this sacred space represent our ecumenical heritage, as many of those names immortalized in the windows are for families who became Episcopal, Lutheran, Baptist, Methodist and Roman Catholic.

There are overlapping stories regarding windows of this era. The first is that the style of these windows are called "patterned windows" related to the iconoclast controversy. Prior to the fame of the Louis Comfort Tiffany Studios of the 1920s in Syracuse, NY, any depiction of human personages in Protestant church windows was considered a violation of the Commandment against fashioning a graven image. It was understood that if humanity is indeed created in the image of God, and the window were to portray an image of a person, then this image was an iconic image portraying God. The 1892 windows were intentionally designed to be abstract pattern designs to avoid any direct images and instead represent patterns found in all creation.

All of the windows have a symbolism related to the Book of Revelation. Above the Pulpit are five small windows, two representing Dogwood in bloom and two representing Persimmons. In the center of the North Chancel Wall is the Cross and Crown an ancient symbol of Christendom, which in post-Modern times has become an image of Reinhold Niebuhr's classic question of Christ and Culture informing without dominating one another.

Among the most dramatic of the windows, the Top Central of the West windows identifies the Alpha and Omega of the Greek Alphabet, that Christ is the Beginning and the End of all we know.

The Top Central of the East windows portrays a Grapevine and clusters, at the center of which is a square box representing the unknown future. When the sunlight passes through the green vines of this window, the effect is to turn the glass a sparkling
gold.

At the center of the Narthex Wall (South) is a shield with a script Letter "C," a Script Letter "A," and the "And/Percent" symbol "&" interwoven. The political controversy of the 1890s was between Presbyterian Calvinism (Predestination) and Unitarian Universalist Arminianism (Free Will); with the "&" symbol emphasizing that God has a Plan for the Universe, but also, we as Human Creatures have Free Will and responsibility to enter in to make a difference, at which point God's Plan unfurls anew.

Stained glass windows were routinely sold by traveling salesmen, selling "patterned windows" out of a catalogue at a lower cost, because they were in regularized abstract patterns. For "special memorials" at a greater cost, families could special order windows depicting more grand designs, as in roses, lilies, the Bible, etc.

The 1892 windows were originally manufactured in Boston, Massachusetts, by the Baird Company, though the receipt and cost of windows has long since been lost to posterity.

All five windows above the Pulpit, were given by sisters-in-law Mrs. Sarah and Julia Hitchcock, in memory of the Hitchcock family.

Following the windows along the East side of the Sanctuary, from North to South:

The Hopkins Window was given by Mrs. T.F. Andrews in memory of her parents: Dr. & Mrs. Judah B. Hopkins.

The Andrews Window was also given by Mrs. T.F. Andrews in memory of her husband Theodore F. Andrews.

The Bartlett Window was given by Edward T. and Lori Bartlett in memory of the Bartlett family.

The Stuart Window is a replacement window, manufactured by the Keck Studios not original to this Sanctuary in 1892, but was given in 1935 in memory of Mr. & Mrs. George Stuart and Mrs. Grace Welling Stuart.

The Thompson/Austin Window was given by sisters'. Orlando J. Austin & Mrs. Peninah Thompson in memory of their husbands, and also of their father Silah Thompson.

The Center Window has no name and no identified donor.

The Leitch Window was given by George & Katherine (Kellogg) Leitch. At the building of the 1831 church, the Kellogg family owned the property to the East of the Church, which now abuts Leitch Avenue.

The Willie Hough Window was given in his memory by his parents, Mr. & Mrs. Thomas Hough.

The Hoagland Window was given by Mrs. Charles Smith and G.W. Hoagland in memory of Alfred Hoagland.

Over the Genesee Street, South doors are 5 windows. The Kelley Window given by Mrs. Thomas Kelley is in memory of her parents, Mr. & Mrs. Chester Patterson.

The Thompson Window was given by Mrs. Charles Goodall, in memory of Peter and Sarah Thompson.

The Austin Window was given in memory of Mr. & Mrs. Warren Austin of Chicago.

The Adams Window was given by Emerson Adams in memory of his parents, Henry and Eliza Adams.

The Cuddeback Window was given by Mrs. Newell Turner in memory of her parents, Mr. & Mrs. Egbert Cuddeback and family.

The round window in the stairway to the Belfry is the Fuller Window, given by Mrs. William Fuller of Chicago, in memory of the Fuller family.

Following the windows on the West side of the Sanctuary, again from North (Chancel) to South:

Cromwell Window was given in memory of Mr. & Mrs. Andrew Ely Cromwell.

The Sloan Window was given by Mr. and Mrs. Augustus T. Sloan of Brooklyn, NY in memory of her mother, Mrs. Caroline Cromwell.

The Hopkins Window was given by Mrs. Elisha Wund Hopkins of Rome, NY in memory of her husband.

The Loveless Window was given by family in memory of M. Eliza Loveless.

The Isbell Window was given in memory of Mr. Charles and Mrs. Harriet (Woodruff) Isbell.

The Wiltsie Window was given by Mrs. A.G. Wiltsie in memory of her husband, Charles and their daughter Grace Wiltsie.

The Austin Window was given by Mrs. Almira Austin in memory of her husband George Austin.

THE 1928 RENOVATIONS

In 1928, Miss Anna H. Allen, the sole surviving member of one of the oldest surviving families of Skaneateles came into a large inheritance. This was a great burden to this quiet woman, who asked the guidance of her attorney. His reply was "Give it away while you are here, to see some of the good it may do." One of her many gifts of philanthropy, was the purchase of the Moeller Pipe Organ for her church, on the condition, that the congregation raise the full amount needed ($11,000) to again bring the whole church into good condition from steeple to cellar, as no work had been done since dedication 1892. What is more, between 1892 and 1928 Plumbing and Electricity had been made available, so this renovation added new utilities which previously had been unavailable. Miss Allen only lived a year after the Dedication of the Organ and Renovations (16 December 1928), but her friends claimed it was the happiest year of her life.

The dining room and kitchen, originally located on the third floor (Kellogg Room) were brought to a new location, immediately North of the Sanctuary. A new heating system was installed. The Chancel (North Wall) of the Sanctuary was physically altered to accommodate the chambers of the new Pipe Organ, as the Johnson Tracker Organ had been located completely within the Sanctuary space, and the Moeller had four separate organ chambers each under expression. The new organ was created by the M.P. Moeller Pipe Organ Company of Hagerstown, Maryland. The organ (without cost of building modifications) was $25,000 in 1928. Miss Anna Allen dedicated the renovation in memory of her brother Phillip Allen who had been a Trustee of the church from 1890 until his death in 1927.

Electric light fixtures replaced gas fixtures, in use from 1892 until 1935. The electric lighting was a gift from Mrs. Kate Hatch in memory of her daughter Elizabeth Hatch. All of the stained-glass windows were re-leaded at this time, with steel rods welded to the lead caning as reinforcing rods.

THE 1950'S ADDITIONS

In 1951 a new addition was added to the North end of the Sanctuary, providing needed classrooms and offices. The design was a flat roofed, single story, brick structure. This addition had two large connected classrooms, plus a library, a meeting board room, along with offices for the pastor and administrative person, as well as restrooms for each sex. This addition was located where in earlier years stables had stood, providing shelter for horses and carriages used for transporting parishioners for worship and meetings.

In 1954, church leaders elected to reclaim the Sanctuary cellar, by removing the rubble of the collapsed 1831 church. Conveyor belts were rigged from the Sanctuary basement through the small half-round cellar windows, while members of the church worked first on hands and knees, then bending over, eventually standing up-right to dig out the 60 years of compacted rubble. When the original floor of the old 1831 Sanctuary was reached, a curious piece of history was unearthed. Beneath all the rubble, timbers, dirt, brick and debris was a slate floor. Underneath several of the pieces of slate, were large open spaces like very shallow graves, large enough to accommodate a person. During the 1860s Abolition Movement, Seneca Falls, Auburn and Skaneateles all had been part of the Underground Railroad for escaping slaves to make their way to Canada. In addition, on the East side of the Cellar was an archway forming the beginning of a tunnel, the other-end of which was a trap door in the porch of the house on the corner of Leitch and

Genesee Streets. It is believed the church had been used as a hiding place of Sanctuary.

The struggles regarding slavery in Skaneateles and throughout Central New York were less among slave owners and abolitionists, and more between those who believed "slavery to be morally wrong" versus those who "desired to take action against slavery". One being theological and philosophical, the latter being activist. According to the official Minutes of the church, one Sunday morning, without prior action or endorsement by Session or pastor, a benevolent offering was taken. Said offering was for the purchase of a single bale of cotton to be shipped to Canada. The Freedmen Offering, became a regular part of the church's benevolent work for several decades until the turn of the Century. It is striking that in all the records of Session Minutes, correspondence from Pastors, prized sermons, there is not a single mention of the Civil War, nor of abolition or slavery.

1952 the Central Schoolhouse in Skaneateles caught fire and was destroyed. Before the last of the flames were out, members of the School Board had begun discussion with each of the local churches to act as temporary classrooms until a new school could be built. The Episcopal, Catholic, Methodist and Presbyterian churches all were put into daily use. For Graduation Ceremonies, from that time until Allyn Arena was built at Austin Park, the Graduating Senior Class sat in the Choir loft of the Sanctuary of the Presbyterian Church, and as their names were called each proceeded out, up the stairs of the Pulpit Dias, receiving their diploma and down the other side.

DOBSON HALL

1959-60 a new Fellowship Hall with Commercial Kitchen and lower level classrooms was constructed as a two-story masonry addition perpendicular and attached to the North end of the 1950's additions. This construction coincident with the impending retirement of the longest pastorate of this church, Rev. John Dobson DD, this addition was dedicated as Dobson Hall. At the time, Dobson Hall provided completion of the church facilities, with the Sanctuary for the worship of God, the Administrative wing for leadership and decision-making, and Dobson Hall for the education and fellowship of Christian believers. In its history, Dobson Hall has provided identity for Boy Scout Troop 61, Skaneateles Early Childhood Center, Mom's & Kids Co-op, Teasletime Before and After School, BOCES Alternative School, Masterworks, and the Skaneateles Garden Club.
1998 Dobson Hall acquired an insulated new roof, thermal windows and new lighting. Suddenly Dobson Hall had a new life as an exhibit hall, the CNY

Quilt Show, local Artisans demonstrating their artwork in an annual juried show, BOCES Student Fairs regularly used the space. 2010 the Session recognized that the floor of Dobson was asbestos, and after 50 years needed replacement. Dr. Lindsey recommended that the new floor encapsulate the old, as well as embodying an ancient spiritual practice of walking The Labyrinth. The design is unique to First Presbyterian Church Skaneateles with a rectangular spiral, at the center of which is the cross. The Labyrinth created some small controversy as one individual was concerned by "new age" spiritualism, but most in the community came to recognize "it is a floor" and for those doing Tai Chi, or Dance, or seeking to reflect and pray, the Labyrinth provides a welcome pattern.

THE ACADEMY STREET MANSE

According to the history of Rev. Mr. Beauchamp of Marcellus, the first manse was located on the edge of the woods, built in 1832. Later (1866), this house was drawn back across the back lots of neighboring properties to be located on East Elizabeth Street. The second parsonage on Academy Street was built in 1905 for Rev. Mr. Edward J. Humeston. This manse was used by families of pastors: Humeston, Rodgers, Vail, Schorge, Fulton, Dobson, Panko, and Eastman. Beginning in 1990, the First Presbyterian Church began providing a housing allowance for pastors to purchase their own home, without the church's responsibilities for maintenance and renovations. In September 1992, the manse on Academy Street was sold for $165,000 and the Manse Fund established in 1997.

THE ORGAN TASK FORCE

The Organ Task Force had been named in 1990, at the height of the Co-Pastorate, including Susan Trowbridge as Chairperson, Jan Fletcher, Steve Frackenpohl, Hugh Hadley, Doug Campbell, with staff members Bunt Osborne (organist) and Tom Baker (Choral Director). The Organ Task Force had been charged with investigating and recommending what could be done with the re-built 1928 Moeller Pipe Organ, or if the instrument were beyond repair to recommend replacement. The Organ Task Force met regularly for seven years, thoroughly investigating the condition of the instrument, as well as electronic instruments, pipe organs of many different designs and manufacturers, as well as the distinction between commissioning a new instrument to be crafted versus purchasing a used classic instrument to be rebuilt. In 1997, the new Pastor met with The Organ Task Force and inquired what more they needed, to be able to make their recommendation. Within the month, the Organ Task Force reported to Session that

> a) the Moeller instrument was beyond repair;
> b) the Organ Task Force recommends purchase of a Pipe Organ over an Electronic instrument both because an electronic instrument provides a reproduction of an Organ's true sound, as well as the anticipated need for replacement of electronic components as compared to a Pipe Organ which with proper maintenance could last for centuries;
> c) that among the instruments considered, contracting for commissioning of a new Organ by the Casavant Freres Pipe Organ Company was the best solution for our church's needs.

The Organ Task Force did however also include an alternative, that if the funding was not possible for this recommendation which was the most expensive option considered, that the Organ Task Force would recommend the purchase of a quality used instrument abandoned from a church to be rebuilt by The John Bishop Firm of Organ Re-Builders. The Session received the Report, thanked the committee for their service and dissolved the Task Force. The Session also recognized that due to the present overlapping capital campaigns, any action on this recommendation would need to wait until the current work and debt situation were resolved.

THE LITURGICAL DESIGN TASK FORCE

The Liturgical Design Task force was created by the Session in the autumn of 1997, after the dissolution of the Organ Task Force, with representation from Susan Trowbridge, Steve Frackenpohl, Sandy Hadley, William Reckmeyer, Susan Meyer, C'leen Hoselton, and staffed by the Pastor Craig Lindsey. First, the Task force received three weeks of Historical Church Architecture and Liturgical Practice teaching from the pastor, regarding the function and purpose of elements of worship setting and practice in Judeo-Christian Reformed Protestant Tradition. The Task Force then were asked to make recommendations for modification of the existing uses of the Sanctuary, rather than completely renovating the Sanctuary. Emphasis became "How to maintain the aura of this traditional holy space, while correcting the current problems of implementation".

The Worship service was streamlined, rather than having multiple points of beginning with Prelude, Announcements, Introit, Call to Worship, Prayer of Invocation, Processional Hymn. The basic order of the Worship service remained unchanged, as this congregation was accustomed to the "traditional style" of building to the sermon. The congregation had a very limited repertoire of hymns, as the former pastor had tended to rotate a dozen favorite hymns over 23 years. The Pastor introduced to the congregation that we would maintain several familiar sacred touch-stones, while being willing to try adaptation at other elements.

Lighting was increased from bare 16 watt flickering incandescent candle-shaped bulbs, to the use of three 150 watt fluorescent bulbs per fixture, diffused through frosted hurricane globes. Hurricane globes were adapted by having the Brennan Stained Glass company sand-blast the belly of clear hurricane globes. By avoiding the top and bottom of the hurricanes from sand-blasting, the glass maintained its tensile strength.

The most dramatic recommendation of the Liturgical Design Task Force included positioning of the proposed new Organ and repositioning of the pews while maintaining their orientation. Rather than the Organ being on the South Wall, or taking up the majority of cubic footage of the newly designed Gathering Space, the Liturgical Design Task Force proposed the Organ straddle the Chancel wall, with the back 6' under expression, and the front 6' being fully exposed and without the ability for expression (shuttering off sound while continuing to play).

Related to the orientation of seating, in the former design, there were four seating sections in the rear of the sanctuary, with three seating sections in the front. Proposal was circulated in the newsletter and annual report, to move the pews into two seating sections with a wide center aisle, all made public before any decision to try this out. The week prior to the first of November (Reformation Sunday) 1997, was one of the most anticipated Sundays on record. Following the Benediction, everyone got down on their hands and knees with screw-guns and electric drills, to unscrew the pews from the floor. A life-sized jigsaw puzzle ensued as all of the pews were removed and throughout the next week, pews were measured and brought back into the Sanctuary to be arranged facing the same direction but with different aisles. The new layout created a central aisle with focus on the central elements of worship The Baptismal Font, the Communion Table and The Pulpit, and done so with no additional cost to the church.

Making changes gradually, the Liturgical Design Task Force recommended that once the congregation became accustomed to the new pew design, then the asbestos flooring and carpet might be replaced with a new oak hardwood flooring, though this meant completely removing the pews and relocating them at least twice. Replacing the flooring took place in March of 2000.

While examining the old floor, the Session learned that a Century of drainage problems had caused several of the supporting timbers to rot. Woodford Brothers was contracted to re-brace, lift and level the floor at a cost of $10,000. There had also been a Choir loft in the Northwest corner of the Sanctuary. The creativity of this loft was that Mottville Chairs each sat upon a tiered platform creating a Wedding cake image for Choir members. However, this loft had been built after the Sanctuary floor had settled, and the loft needed to be removed in order to straighten, level and stabilize the floor. M&D Flooring actually removed the asbestos and replaced the floor with North Carolina red oak, then finished the floor at a cost of $15,000. While an expensive undertaking, this preemptive action avoided repeating the tragedy of a hundred years prior, when the 1831 Sanctuary was lost to rotting support columns. On the Sunday in between the two weeks of pew removal and re-installation, the congregation worshiped in Dobson Hall with great cooperation and enthusiasm. The ornamental aisle runner arrived a few weeks later, having been handmade and imported from Brussels. The aisle runner served a dual purpose of carrying the eye of the worshiper to the Chancel, as well as absorbing water and slush from the boots of worshipers entering from outdoors.

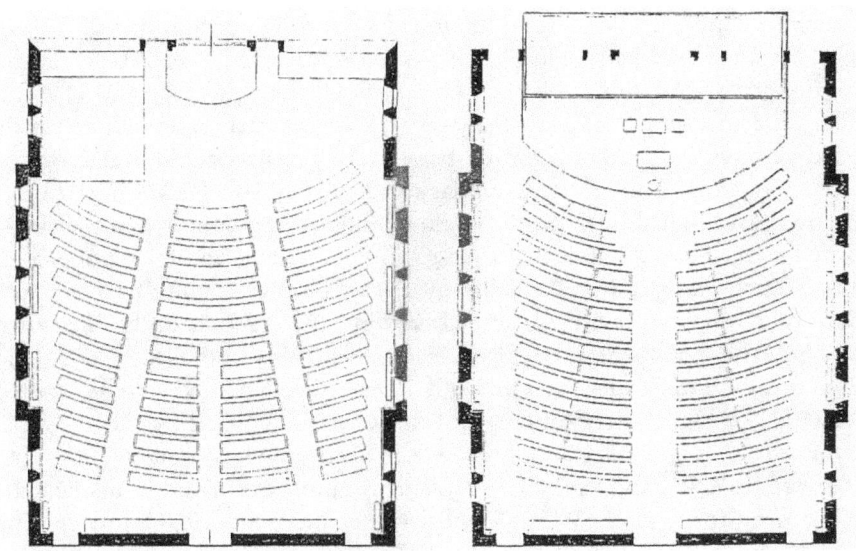

THE ALL CHURCH TASK FORCE

In 1994, the Rev. Dr. Steve Thomas was elected by the Session to serve as Interim Pastor. This was a turbulent time in the life of the church, guiding the congregation through the processes of grieving and transition following the retirement of Rev. Dr. Earle Eastman, the healing of several divisions brought about by an ill-conceived Co-Pastorate to avoid an Interim, and the essential groundwork of naming issues to prepare the church for the Call of the next installed pastor, Rev. Craig Lindsey. At their first Session meeting with Rev. Dr. Thomas, Elders Jim Wayne (Building and Grounds) and Brent Ward (Finance) informed the new Interim Pastor of the need to address major building issues. Dr. Thomas then attempted to inform the Session that Building Campaigns were not the work of Interim Ministry, in fact he had no training of experience in Building or Capital Campaigns. At which point Jim Wayne placed an old brick on the Table stating that this had been pulled out of the exterior wall, as there was no mortar holding the church together any longer.

An All Church Task Group was created, composed of Mrs. Linda Keenan, Mrs. Ellie Tucker, Paul Vaivoda and Dick Grambow. This All Church Task Group identified needs for handicap accessibility, energy conservation, improved drainage, improved lighting, classroom spaces, offices and community utilization of the building.

In addition, the bell in the Southwest tower was in dangerous need of new structural support. The 1952 addition had a flat roof, which routinely leaked, as well as accumulating leaves and seed-pods which would germinate requiring the roof to be mowed. The roofs of the Sanctuary and Dobson Hall were in excess of thirty years old. The Sanctuary basement routinely filled with ground water. The foundation of the Center addition had settled separately from that of the Sanctuary and of Dobson Hall. The Dobson Fellowship Hall had been constructed without any insulation, and the single paned metal framed windows provided little barrier to wind, let alone cold. The Stained-glass windows installed a Century before were in such desperate need of renovation that the glass was bowing and cracking under their own weight. The main entrance of the church offices and classrooms (and therefore of the church) was through a small wooden shed attached to the west side of the church, looking not unlike an outhouse privy. The overall layout of the building had been re-muddled and added to so many times that every space felt dark, cramped, broken up and systematically inadequate. After over forty years of neglected maintenance, the 1928 Moeller Pipe Organ had needed re-leathering in 1970. Instead, plans were adopted to rebuild the instrument from a Germanic style to a French Baroque. Tragically, those involved did not use the factory manufacturers, but accepted the cheapest bid without verifying references. The Organ Re-Builder lived in the church for two years while rebuilding the instrument. On occasion, this meant the church smelled of liver and onions, while on other occasions, the technician was found wandering through the church only partially dressed. Amid many allegations, he was let go. Only at that time, was it learned that rather than precision re-tooling of the pipes, he had used a box-cutter blade and needle-nosed pliers to twist the metal as he thought it should be. In the end, the instrument was ruined. Twenty years later in the 1990s, the wind chests and leather which had never been replaced developed significant leaks, causing the instrument to sound like running water from escaping air. Professional Organ Tuners anticipated the instrument's complete failure within the decade, and in fact the instrument had caught fire more than once. When all these needs were joined, the projected costs grossly exceeded one million dollars. Given the circumstance of the congregation at this time, that potential seemed overwhelming to the congregation.

RE-LEADING THE STAINED-GLASS WINDOWS

Among the first specific gifts for major maintenance was titled Maintenance & Repair Fund, and was used for re-Leading the Stained-Glass Windows. Overtime, the weight of the glass had pushed the soft lead caning, allowing the windows to belly and bow. Eventually, glass surpasses a point of bending and shatters, however many of the shades of glass used are no longer available for manufacture due to the high lead content. This endowment provided for a few windows each year to be removed, broken shards to be replaced, and the windows remade in multiple sections with the weight of the glass segregated and diffused to the window frames by flat horizontal steel bars. Cost of the renovation of each of the 34 windows was $2,000 to $ 5,000 per window. The Brennan Stained Glass Company of Syracuse was one of the successor companies to the Tiffany Studio, and has undertaken this project.

THE RENOVATION STEERING GROUP 1994-1996

Due to the total cost estimates for bidding exceeding $1,000,000 a decision was made to stratify the work into separate phases, dealing with the most critical structural repair issues first, then replacement of the center building with new layout and design-work, and only after this was completed to consider what to do about the organ concern which had become highly politicized. The Renovation Steering Group was created to oversee the work of renovation. The Renovation Steering Group (RSG) was composed of Mrs. Connie Brace-Higman (a local architect) as Chair, Elder Bill Stevens (a Project Manager with Niagara Mohawk Utility) as Session representative, Paul Vaivoda (independent architect), Bob Chaffee (small business owner), Jan Sterling (Presbyterian Women's Association), Joe Hubbard (a retired handyman and subsistence farmer), and Dick Grambow (a Veterinarian and horticulturist). Created immediately following the dissolution of the Co-Pastorate, continuing through rediscovery of buried sexual abuses from the past, and the Call of a new Pastor, these were highly-polarized times, and RSG often exerted power and authority, over what would and would not happen, in what priority. The first phase of work was intended to tuck-point the masonry of the most critical portions of the buildings (in total 45% of the buildings); reinforce the structure of the bell tower, and rebuild the bell cradle; extend the Sanctuary gable twenty-feet to the North, beyond the peak of the second transept gable, to protect the Chancel wall and Pipe Organ from run-off; to install a French Drain around the perimeter for the building to keep ground water from entering the building; to refinish the Genesee Street doors; and to replace all roofs. Phase Two would be to hire an Architect, to design a new Center Building. Phase Three included an independent group titled the Organ Task Force, who researched what kind of instrument to replace the Pipe Organ and what costs might be.

CAPITAL FUND I 1995-2000

A separate committee was formed to do fund raising, and because no one at that time had experience with Fund Raising the Presbyterian Foundation was contracted to lead the campaign. Campaign Fund I Committee was composed of Jack Capron (Chairperson), Larry Pickett, Dave Graham, Doug Campbell, Steve White, Brent Ward, Diane Ward, Cheryl Clark, Hugh Hadley, Lynn Ralph, Gardner McLean, Phyllis Clark and Jim Wayne. While the committee set out to raise $350,000 across 5 year pledges, the congregation surprised itself by pledging $500,000 for Capital Fund I (1995-1999). The program design from Presbyterian Foundation provided the content of letters and plan for elaborate pledge dinners at the Country Club, however the actual cost of these events and mailings, and the work involved all needed to be done by the church leaders and staff. Cost of the Foundation for the Campaign was an additional 10% of the funds raised ($50,000), plus the congregation needed to pledge an another 10% ($50,000) for mission giving. Therefore, the $500,000 pledged over 1995-2000 would net $400,000 to Building Repair.

RENOVATION STEERING GROUP II 1997-98 RSG II

While the dramatic renovations of tuck-pointing and re-roofing of RSG I were going on outdoors, the Renovation Steering Group was hard at work on the Design Stage of Phase II. A Rochester based architectural firm, Doran Yarrington, was hired to consider energy efficiency, handicap accessibility, more appropriate lay-out and consistent design, taking into account the difference between the elevation of the Sanctuary and the elevations of the two stories of Dobson Hall, in creating a new middle connecting building. The solution became location of an elevator immediately adjacent to the Sanctuary building, allowing the middle section to approximate the two-story elevation of Dobson Hall, thereby making the church like a split-level house. While this afforded twice the square footage of the former Center Building, the costs were also increased to double what had been projected for replacement of the 1952 building addition.

A grand new entrance was also to be designed for the West Entrance to the church, entering off the parking lot. Because of the grandeur of this new entrance, the architect recommended turning the Sanctuary a full 180 degrees, for the congregation to face toward Genesee Street. The congregation was now divided anew, by those willing to change, and those committed to what they had always known to be true. Added to this discussion, were concerns about accommodating automobile transportation, when the Sanctuary had been built in an era of horse and buggy transit that might change again; while the Organ Task Force were concerned for the potential location of a new Pipe Organ.

In November 1996, the RSG reported to the congregation that because there were too many controversies at the time (not the increased cost), the RSG had dictated that Phase II Renovations could not include both replacement of the Center Building, problems in Dobson Hall, and problems in the Sanctuary with the Pipe Organ. The congregation were asked to choose which of these three sections was of greatest need, because everything could not be done. While the congregation was of a diverse and divisive plurality, replacement of the Center Building was declared to have received more un-official votes than either the Pipe Organ or Dobson Hall renovations. Therefore, like the division of a room between contesting siblings, a bold, blood-red 6" wide red line was drawn in the hallway, cutting off the Sanctuary from the Center Building. At the other end, the change of elevation to Dobson Hall and perimeter doors defined the barrier.

Simultaneous to these decisions, in January of 1996 buried rumors of sexual abuse from a pastor 40 years prior began to surface. The Interim Pastor, Session and Presbytery began work of investigating what harm had been done to whom, decades before, then prosecuting the former pastor, all amid an air of secrecy and conflict. The impact of this abuse cannot be over-stated, because while the culprit was removed as pastor, later prosecuted and he chose to retire with full pension by renouncing the authority of his Ordination vows; for every member of the church and staff and future pastors boundaries and roles, power, faith and authority all were confused.

A small but significant change was made to the RSG building design at this time. In every office and classroom door there are now windows. In the 1892 design, pride had been taken that every door include panels to form the shape of the cross. In the 1997 renovation, windows in doors allow there to be confidentiality of what is said, while maintaining that those on the other side of the door always realize that they can be witnessed. The church is and needs to be a place of sanctuary and safety, tragically in the times we live in, that same sanctuary must be guarded by safeguards. Thus, every doorway reminds us both of The Cross of Jesus, as well as the abuses and secrets which will no longer be tolerated in the church.

The new Pastor was elected the last weekend in September, with plans for arrival, purchase of a new home for his family, moving into their home, leading worship on Sunday (two days before Christmas 1996), all in the midst of a Building Campaign, Building Renovations, a rediscovered Secret of violated trusts and abuses by clergy, rumor of the prosecution of a former pastor, and one of the former pastors living in the community.

CAPITAL FUND II

The Capital Fund II Committee included Bob Chaffee, Bill Allyn, Doug

Rutan and the new Pastor. To try to get to know the congregation and determine the values and limitations of the church's assets, the new Pastor Rev. Craig Lindsey read all of the existent Wills and Estates and the full Minutes of the Church beginning in quill pen in 1801. Two questions were raised by this review, which have continued to weigh upon the Finance Committee and the Session. Several of the Wills and Estates were originally given to the church in the 1800s and 1900s, without specific dedication other than: "for the future of the church". Confronted with a significant capital renovation, 150 – 200 years after the gift, is this now the future time that was intended, or did the donor intend a perpetuity without expenditure of principal under any circumstance? Second, as gifts may be invested for growth or for interest income, does the Session have authority to spend all growth, or only the interest income on investments?

By the summer of 1997, only six months after the arrival of the new pastor, architectural designs of RSG Phase II were ready for submission to the Skaneateles Historical Commission for comment and approval. The Village Historical Commission met with the Pastor and members of the RSG seven times over as many months to modify designs, paying particular attention to the new entry, whether the shape of windows was the same as historic ones, the depth of architectural shadow details, the color of brick, the color of trim and the color and composition of mortar.

The congregation was then asked to pledge the Second Building Campaign for 1997-2000 totaling an estimated $850,000 to cover the costs of rebuilding the Center section. Recognize, that the membership was pledging a three-year Campaign for $850,000, while simultaneously paying the final three years of their first campaign for $500,000, while also being asked to increase their pledges to the Annual Operating Budget by 10% compounded per year, following the leadership of a pastor under 40 years of age, who had been installed for less than a year. In 1997, The First Presbyterian Church of Skaneateles was recognized with "The Excellence in Evangelism" Award by the General Assembly of the Presbyterian Church USA, for being the fastest growing congregation in the Synod of the Northeast.

THE PURPOSE OF REBUILDING

As the new Pastor and Congregation began work together in December 1996, they began fresh discussion of the reasons why, for wanting to make these renovations. While there were immediate expressions of the need for a roof that does not leak, for energy efficiency to reduce bills, and a pipe organ that does not gush wind, underlying these were a desire to keep up with the other churches in the Village to remain current. Listening, Rev. Lindsey named a new and different vision for making the building more useable:

> "This church, First Presbyterian Church, could become more visible, more vital and active, could again become a community center for positive activities in the community. Explicit in this is that *we use the church resources as a mission in this local community* rather than standing vacant until Sunday mornings. All of which could also add to the revenues of the church, but at the cost of others using our church, which **challenges our concept of our church being "ours."**"

Within a year after building renovations, the church was in use, every portion of every day of the week, throughout the year. As early as 6am children in 3rd through 5th grades were dropped off at the church by working parents, for a school bus to pick the children up at 8:30am. From 8am until 3pm five days a week, youth in 6th through 8th grades, who had been expelled from the regular public school program, received standard education with specialized teachers in highly supervised smaller classrooms, through the BOCES Alternative School program. As many as 30 students in 6 classes of five, remained current with their academic training, in three 3 hour programs per day. Again after-school, 3rd to 5th Graders returned for Teasel-time's After School Care until 6pm. Weekly, Moms & Kids Co-op provided structured play supervision, with parents volunteering one week, in exchange of others watching their infants and toddlers for three weeks, as well as learning parenting skills and support. Martial Arts classes offered teaching of focus, discipline and spirituality. Tai Chi, Yoga and Weight Training classes strengthened the bodies and spirits, developing a specialization for persons recovering from heart disease surgery to re-learn balance and coordination. Tap, Jazz and Ballet classes, Painting classes, Music lessons, all took place in the Presbyterian church. Onondaga Pastoral Counseling, along with independent counselors rented space. The American Red Cross began offering community Blood Drives at the church every month. Beginning in 2000, Skaneateles Festival had their year-round offices in one of the lower level classrooms, their Board meetings in the Conner Room and for the month of August, the Sanctuary was used as the Community Concert Hall for Grammy Award Winning Chamber Musicians.

CONSTRUCTION FINANCING

When plans for financing a second Capital Campaign simultaneous to the repayment of the first Capital Campaign, while dramatically increasing the Operating Budget, were shared with the Session for adoption, there was a good deal of doubt. The Session member on the Renovation Steering Group created a possible projection that after 30 years, the church would be at least $100,000 in debt. The Finance Chairperson on Session anticipated that after 50 years, the church would still be in debt. All the while, the Pastor and the Business Administrator/Treasurer assured the Session that within three years, all debt from these campaigns would be satisfied.

Rather than contracting for Fund-raising, Rev. Lindsey guided the campaign, himself. Working with the support of the WD Burdick Co. drafting the copy, compiling the promotional book which explained the campaign, and managing the campaign. Doing these services "in-house" saved the church an additional $85,000 in administrative costs (10%).

Rev. Lindsey completed four separate application documents for the General Assembly of the Presbyterian Church (USA) for: Handicap Accessibility; for Installation of an Elevator; for Asbestos Abatement; and for New Construction. At the January 1998 meeting the local Presbytery endorsed these loans, which were then reviewed and endorsed by the Synod of the Northeast in February 1998, for General Assembly approval on the first of March. Each of these loans were to provide short-term financing, while the members of the church fulfilled pledges, to allow the work to proceed immediately and without interruption. In the long-term, if needed, these loans were anticipated to be rolled into one 30-year commercial mortgage. However, on Good Friday 1998, Rev. Lindsey was informed by a letter, misaddressed and delivered to the Episcopal Church across the Street, that the PCUSA General Assembly Committee had REJECTED all of these loans and their financing. A new policy had been established, during this meeting of this General Assembly Committee, stating that loans could not be combined, and the maximum total now available for GA Loans was now $300,000. Further, a member of the GA Review Committee had vacationed in Skaneateles recently, and recommended that this community was "too affluent" to need a denominational loan. All financing was therefore CANCELLED, two days prior to Ground Breaking on Easter morning.

Over Easter weekend, Rev. Lindsey scrambled to meet with the newly arrived Presbytery Executive Rev. David Johnson and the newly appointed Synod of the Northeast Associate for Congregational Development Rev. Dr. N. Scott Cupp. Lindsey made the case that because the Presbytery and Synod had acted to support Loans from the General Assembly, the Synod and Presbytery were responsible for guaranteeing the loans. Between Good Friday and Easter morning he had secured an alternative combination of loans and loan guarantees from the Synod of the Northeast to cover the financing. These loans were established at 6.5% interest with the provision that annually the rates would adjust.

The morning after Easter 1998, while the pastor was signing documents and concluding negotiations on financing, the contractors began the work of asbestos abatement, wetting down and removing both asbestos floor tiles and their asbestos based adhesive, asbestos heating pipe insulation, and extremely friable asbestos wallboard lining an oil-fired boiler room at an unanticipated cost of $100,000. One week later, the bulldozer began demolition.

There are always those in congregations who are saints, silently going about their work without wanting attention. As demolition work began, the leadership suddenly recognized that the church building had three separate heating systems: A Natural Gas Boiler system for the Sanctuary; a second Natural Gas Boiler system for Dobson Hall; and a third Oil burning Boiler system for the Center Building. This third Boiler system was in a small room lined with highly friable asbestos which had to be removed at a cost of $100,000 which the Architect had not taken into account. As this hazardous waste was being removed, it suddenly occurred to the Pastor that the Annual Operating Budget of the Church included costs for Gas, Electricity, Water and Sewer, but there had been no cost for Heating Oil. One of the members of the church whose business was the sale and delivery of Heating Oil, had for several decades, routinely stopped at the church to empty the balance of their delivery truck into the church's oil tank for free, which had provided 100% of the fuel for this Boiler. How many decades this had taken place, how much they had contributed, was never requested to be credited or repaid.

The most amazing part of all the renovations was the support of this congregation. Recovering from the division of the church in conflict from a co-pastorate and discovery of buried clergy sexual abuse, with a new pastor, still the congregation simultaneously paid:

> five year pledges for $850,000 on Campaign I
> during the last three years of this, simultaneously paid pledges for an additional $1,250,000
> plus the unanticipated costs of asbestos abatement $100,000
> plus unanticipated floor lifting and bracing and replacement of the Sanctuary floor
> plus restoration of the Stained Glass Windows
> plus Dobson Hall replacement of thermal pane matching new windows
> plus new Dobson Hall Roof, with new decking, 6" of insulation and roofing
> in addition Session asked to increase giving to the Annual Operating Budget for Program, Staffing and Mission by 10 – 15% compounded each of the years 1997, 1998, 1999, 2000
> and the congregation oversubscribed giving by a surplus of $10,000 to $20,000 per year.

The added funds empowered the Session to assist in giving additional dollars to mission and to prepayment of principal on the loans to repay the debt more quickly.

When projected costs of renovations had been shared with the congregation in 1994, the total cost estimate was $1,100,000 and the congregation scoffed that this could never be done. In 1996 square footage was then doubled. The General Assembly cancelled all loan applications, however the church was able to acquire loan guarantees for up to 30 years which were then repaid within 3 years. In total, $1,250,000 was spent on Phase II renovations; $2,100,000 for the two phases together; saving a projected minimum of $2,500,000 in future interest charges.

DOBSON HALL REBUILDING

While the RSG and Session had recommended (November 1996) that this renovation only deal with the Center building, by the summer of 1997 the new Pastor proposed to Session that the congregation could consider additional concerns. In addition the church's long term costs and renovation would be greatly reduced by addressing Dobson Hall's problems with energy efficiency, lack of insulation and replacement of windows, while the roof and windows of the Center building were being replaced. Six inches of polystyrene insulation between composite strand-boards were attached to the roof decking of Dobson Hall and a new roof laid over the whole. When the double pane insulated glass windows replaced the aluminum frame single pane windows, the panels were in so much larger sections as to make the windows appear larger over all. While this added to the overall project costs, this avoided repeating elements of the project. The original lighting in Dobson Hall had been installed in 1960. Lighting studies were completed and the three 60 watt incandescent fixtures were replaced with six fluorescent bulb fixtures along with perimeter halogen lighting fixtures, at the same electrical usage with a cost for relighting of $30,000.

THE CHURCH IN TRANSITION

During these renovations, the Narthex entrance of the Sanctuary became the church office. Rev. Lindsey used the Bell Tower stairs as a bookshelf, while Business Administrator/Treasurer Gail Banks used the East Carriage Entrance Tower as her office, while the center section provided space for office machines and visitors. Liturgically, the Narthex of a church was originally the place believers atoned for their sins prior to entering the Sanctuary of God. Having the church offices in the Narthex provided a new context for church administration. The availability of having the Sanctuary doors open for visitors, having the offices "on the street", and having the view of the lake during the summer, made these "summer offices" a great treat. Having the offices here also allowed the congregation access to the staff without crossing the construction site, while allowing the staff to closely supervise the progress of construction. Rev. Lindsey could often be found walking the construction site, wearing a construction hard hat marked "REV," blessing every stage of construction.

Throughout the spring and summer of 1998, all of the committees, the Deacons, the Session, met in the Sanctuary. The Session extended tables across the Sanctuary Chancel, with the Communion Table at the center of their work. Having several of the committees meeting simultaneously in the same space, allowed the committees to recognize the importance of one another's work. Meeting in the Sanctuary empowered the Session and committees to affirm the business of the church is one form of serving Christ.

Among all the committee members who worked on these renovations, three volunteers deserve to be mentioned. Renovation Steering Group Chairperson Connie Brace and Paul Vaivoda, each professional architect, offered wisdom and suggestions that prevented problems more often than anyone could count. Elder William Stevens became Project Manager for the renovation. Mr. Stevens rechecked specifications, took his own measurements, approved every change order personally and demanded the highest quality from the contractors. The Diamond Thiel Construction Company were the General Contractors for the job. These professionals gave their very best, made certain the work was done in a timely manner, went out of their way to do little things like wetting down the job site to keep down the dust for neighbors, and months afterward continued to return to make corrections when necessary.

THE CHURCH'S PASTORS

The following descriptions of the Pastors of the First Presbyterian Church was penned by Rev. O.L. White for the Centennial of the church in 1901.

The Rev. Mr. Swift was the church's first pastor. He was installed in 1811, a full decade after the organization of the church. However, the congregation, accustomed to traveling missionaries, who preached a few good sermons then moved on, soon found fault (probably justifiably according to the Session Minutes), and Rev. Swift remained only a little over a year.

The Rev. Benjamin Rice from Massachusetts was the second pastor, 1813 until 1817.

He was then followed by Rev. B.B. Stockton, who remained five years until 1822.

Rev. Alexander Cowan from Virginia was installed and began a troublesome career in 1822. Notwithstanding his "southern prejudices and characteristics," which appear to have been unacceptable and objectionable to the congregation, he remained installed pastor until 1828.

In 1828, The Rev. Mr. S.W. Brace was installed, and continued as pastor until 1843. His pastorate of fifteen years was a momentous and prosperous period in the church's history, highlighted by the construction of the 1831 church building, and sale of the first church to the Baptist Association. It was also during Rev. Brace's tenure that the Manse was purchased in 1832 at a cost $1,800. The same house still stands, though considerably changed. A new church had been organized by the time our second church was built – St. James Episcopal Church – and they erected their first church building in 1827.

Succeeding Rev. Brace came Rev. Samuel Bush. Rev. Bush was installed 1844 - 1851.

The Rev. Sheldon Haynes was installed in 1851. He had been an attorney before entering seminary and the ordained ministry, and was a man of exceptional intellect. However, during his ministry the church experienced tumultuous times, as the interests of the church, and the work of the church, were confined to cases of Church Discipline. Rev. Haynes remained from 1851 until 1855, yet within these four years the church experienced 19 Disciplinary Trials.

In 1856, The Rev. W.B. Dada was ordained and installed as pastor immediately after graduation from Auburn Theological Seminary. Rev. Dada was described as "the venerable father of the Presbytery of Syracuse", though he remained here at Skaneateles only two years, and his labors were remembered as a blessing to all.

In 1859 Rev. A. Mandell arrived from Westernville, Oneida County, NY. Mr. Mandell also remained but two years.

In 1862 The Rev. M. N. Preston came for his first Call directly from Auburn Theological Seminary. His pastorate of twenty-two years was the longest up until then, in the history of this church. During these years, the church enjoyed steady and substantial growth. This was also the period of the great and terrible Civil War and subsequent Southern Reconstruction.

In October 1885 Rev. E.G. Cheeseman was Called to the First Presbyterian Church Skaneateles, beginning his labors 01 November 1885. Rev. Cheeseman however was never installed as pastor, as his health became increasingly poor, and 27 July 1886, only nine months after his arrival, he died while on vacation in Webster, NY. In all the history of this church, Rev. Cheeseman was the only pastor to have died during his ministry here. Memorial services were greatly attended, on 22 August 1886.

The following 1st of February 1887, Rev. O.L. White began and continued in ministry here through his retirement in 1904.

In total, there had been twelve pastorates in the first hundred years of the church, the longest of which was 22 years, two had lasted 15 years each, and the most brief was cut to a short 9 months by death.

The second hundred years has added another dozen pastors, one of which for 28 years, another for 22 years. These second hundred years brought the advent of professional Interim Pastors, who similar to our first missionaries stay only a brief time, leaving no footprints while attempting to furrow the soil for fresh growth and harvest. While there have been these exceptions of two pastorates of 22 years and one of 28 years, the most common duration in two hundred years (15 of the 24 pastors) has been only two to four years. While the "chronological" ascription of dates only serves to determine what happened before or after; the 20th Century in North America experienced great cultural and social change, wars to end all wars, inventions of technology and communication, the transiency of people, shifting priorities, ethics and morals, as well as changes in the styles of pastoral ministry and issues of Christian concern.

For 22 months, 1904-1906, the Rev. E.L. Humeston was installed pastor, during which the Manse on Academy Street was built.

The church was without pastoral leadership 1906-1907.

In 1907, Rev. John Rodger was installed.

Five years later, Rev. Rodger was replaced by Rev. Alfred Vail who served for seven years, seven years marked by the first World War, Rev. Vail accepting a new call in 1919.

From 1920 through 1933, the enacting of Prohibition, the Great Economic Depression, and Women in America receiving the Vote, Rev. F.C. Scorge served as pastor. During Rev. Scorge's Pastorate, initiated by a gift from Mrs. Anna Allen in memory of her brothers, the church installed electricity and indoor plumbing, a new kitchen, new oil fueled heating plant, a new Pipe Organ, and the first re-leading of the Stained-glass windows installed in 1891.

Rev. Albert Fulton served as pastor for five years 1933-1938, during which Sanctuary lighting was changed from gas sconce fixtures and chandeliers to electric lighting in many of the same fixtures. Also during the pastorate of Rev. Fulton, Mrs. Louise Fell Klump began as Church Organist, with Mrs. Howlett as Director of Music. Descendants of the Howlett and Klump families continue in membership of this church through the date of this publication (2017).

In 1938, the Rev. Dr. John Dobson began a 27-year ministry. Dr. Dobson is reverently remembered, as a tall and lanky man. He was responsible for guiding the merger of the Women's Foreign Mission Society and Ladies Aid Society into the United Presbyterian Women; for creation of Standing Committees of the church; and for instituting monthly Session meetings with Elders serving rotating three year terms, rather than meeting annually and being installed for life. Rev. Dobson led this congregation in ministry through WWII, the expansion of suburbs, the Assassination of President John F. Kennedy. Within this church, Rev. Dobson also led the building of the one-story Center building addition, the use of the churches and Grange after the School Fire, the building of Dobson Hall, incurring of mortgage debt, the hiring of Lib Harst as Church Secretary, and when Mrs. Klump had a heart attack the hiring of her nephew Bunt Osborne as Organist in 1965. Bunt Osborne's mother, Mrs. Gertrude Osborne, the sister to Mrs. Klump had been hired as Director of Music in 1950 and she continued in this capacity until 1975.

Dr. John Dobson retired in 1965, and after six months of travel moved into a new home also located on Academy Street. Dr. Dobson continued to attend and participate as Pastor Emeritus until his death in 1994.

1965 until 1970 Steve Panko served as Pastor. The late 1960s in North America were a time of Social Change, it was the time of Civil Rights protests, the Viet Nam War, it was also a time of exploring relationship boundaries and moral codes. During Mr. Panko's ministry here the church expanded in youth ministry with weekly dances in Dobson Hall, Youth Discussion groups and Fellowships, the hiring of Rev. David Becker as Assistant Pastor. In these four years 236 new members joined the church for a total of 700. Suddenly one Sunday morning, there was a Special Congregational Meeting for dissolution of the pastorate. There was no explanation "Why?" and at least half of the congregation did not know why. That year 224 members left the church membership.

The Rev. Earle Eastman arrived in 1970. For the interview, he flew his own plane from his former pastoral Call in Palmyra, NY to the Aerodrome on the west-side of Skaneateles. Rev. Eastman described his Call at Skaneateles, as quieting things down and resolving problems of the church behind closed doors. Session meetings throughout Rev. Eastman's pastorate often ran until past Midnight, particularly when discussing the Co-Pastorate. Dr. Eastman often told the story, that following his first Session meeting here he came home as his wife Jane was preparing to unpack the last box. He told her to stop, because he was not certain how long this would last. Throughout his years in Skaneateles he kept that un-opened box moved from previous homes.

Rather than Retire, seek another Call, or continue in ministry solo, Dr. Eastman encouraged that the church and Presbytery call a co-Pastor to share in this ministry beginning in 1989.

Rev. George Taylor came from Long Island, and he and Rev. Eastman were then co-Pastors from 1989 until 1992. This was not a good pairing, and conflict between the two spread to the congregation. Alban Institute's professional Conflict Resolution Team were contracted to work with the church, but after numerous interviews, when Alban Institute prepared to make their final report, Dr. Eastman announced his retirement to live in this community. The Presbytery then directed Rev. Taylor that he had a year to find a new Call.

The Rev. Dr. Steve Thomas came as a professional Interim, experienced with Conflict circumstances. During Rev. Thomas' 22 months in Skaneateles, he helped the congregation to name the conflict and to recognize that it was not enough to have removed Rev. Panko for abuse, he continued to abuse other congregations for thirty years, and those abused were never able to process their grief because their congregation had not listened to them.

Rev. Craig Lindsey came to Skaneateles in December of 1996, arriving Saturday, preaching two services Sunday, with two different worship services on Monday evening, Christmas Eve. The congregation which when he arrived began at 360 members grew to over 700 in spite of regular cleaning of membership rolls. In 2016 the Session redefined membership versus friends of the church, settling on a membership of about 500 with over 200 friends of the church who support the church, call this their church home, but do not reside locally throughout the year. From 2001 until 2003, Rev. Lindsey earned his Doctor of Ministry degree at Columbia Seminary in Atlanta, all of the coursework, Doctoral project and Thesis, were directly correlated to understanding this congregation. In 2016-2017, Dr. Lindsey enrolled in a psychiatric counseling program through the Bowen Center at George Washington University in Washington, DC. Bowen Family Systems theory is unique, in that rather than focusing on treatment of the patient out of context, the identified patient is understood as party of a family system; in addition, rather than a utopian ideal of "normal," "normal" is understood as being whatever is normal for that family. Because of this, when the identified patient begins to question or make changes, the other family members have an investment in keeping the individual as they were, because this protects their identities and relationships, power, and sense of what is normal. Rev. Dr. Lindsey began work on understanding the church, which often identifies itself as being a church-family, as being treated as a Family System.

In June of 2014, Mario Bolivar was Ordained and Installed in his first Call as our Associate Pastor. Mario was originally from Barranquilla, Colombia, who trained as an Attorney before going to Seminary. While a natural outgrowth, needed by the church in leadership, Calling an Associate Pastor to work with the installed Pastor was a bold move as the church had been wounded previously by being divided between two pastors, but this time there was a hierarchy, differing responsibilities, and intentional sensitivity from the senior pastor.

From Rev. Rice consistently through Rev. John Dobson, all of the pastors had been alumni of Auburn Theological Seminary. Auburn Theological Seminary, located in the neighboring City of Auburn, NY was the only seminary ever to have been associated with a Synod (NY) instead of being associated with the General Assembly of the Presbyterian Church. Auburn Seminary closed in 1918 and merged with Union Theological Seminary on the Upper Westside of New York City. Union being an ecumenical, non-denomination graduate school of religion, all graduates who are Presbyterian are automatically considered alumni of Auburn Theological Seminary. Steven Panko graduated from Union Seminary in New York City. Rev. Dr. Earle Eastman and Rev. George Taylor each graduated from Princeton Theological Seminary. Rev. Dr. Steve Thomas graduated from Union Theological Seminary at Richmond, VA. Rev. Dr. Craig Lindsey earned his Masters in Divinity from Union Theological Seminary in New York City, and earned his Doctorate from Columbia Theological Seminary in Atlanta, GA. Associate Pastor Mario Bolivar attended United Theological Seminary, a United Methodist Seminary in Ohio.

THE TRIALS AND TRIBULATIONS OF THE CHURCH

According to Rev. O.L. White, who was pastor of the church at the First Centennial celebration of 1901, these years were marred with church trials and the settling of differences. The regular church Minutes begin in 1810 with a Case of Church Discipline. The church having begun as a Religious Society to adjudicate conflicts within the community, nearly every difference of opinion between neighbors seems to have been brought before the Session. If a man was seen intoxicated, driving a cow or flock of sheep across any pasture than his own, someone would bring accusation to the church, and the defendant would need to state his case, giving his reasons before the Session, or else fear excommunication and shunning within the Village.

PROFESSORS OF RELIGION

Insofar as members of the church became such by making a public profession of religion, emphasis was placed upon the public identity and moral character of the one professing, rather than upon the grace of God, or the responsibilities of church membership. In "Disciplinary Trials" offenses were characterized as "heresies committed by professors of religion." Public intoxication or swearing publicly, were perceived as being equal public representations of the moral character and professions of an individual as declaring love of Jesus Christ as Lord and Savior.

There were two particularly long and vigorously contested trials within this church, gaining great notoriety. The first was of "a man who had taken the Name of the Lord in vain while present in the Sanctuary of the Church." He had committed "falsehood against his brother by refusing to tell the truth, when accused of public drunkenness." For well over a year the Session interviewed witnesses and privately prayed about this matter, while exhorting the individual to confess, both to his drunkenness, to his bearing false witness in testimony of Jesus Christ in a Disciplinary Trail of the church, and finally in his committing blasphemy against the name of the Lord in the House of the Lord. After being removed from the rolls of the church, he was re-instated in order to be transferred to the rolls of another church. A short-time after his transfer of membership, the gentleman wrote a letter to the Session, claiming he did not truly understand why they had taken these actions against him, as in his own conscience he had done nothing sinful.

The second trial concerned a woman "professor", whose father owned a local drinking tavern and inn. The woman was witnessed crawling through the window of a room in the inn, in the dark of night, into the bedchamber of a man who was not her husband. At the first trial, the woman refused to appear before the Session. Judged to be guilty she was removed from the communicant rolls. However, several weeks later, she did appear before the Session, in recognition of her presence to testify, she was re-instated as a member and professor of the Christian truth. Yet, in the course of her testimony, she was found to have made enough false statements, lies and blasphemies that she was again removed from the rolls.

In those days, to be removed from the rolls of the church meant ex-communication. Those who were ex-communicated not only endured public disgrace, they were denied participation in communion, they were publicly shunned, and upon death could not be buried on church soil. Consider the power of these acts regarding relationship for those considered to be professors of truth and faith. The grace of God was publicly revoked from them as disgrace. Insofar as the sharing of the Sacrament of Communion was perceived to be a complete openness and sharing, absolute forgiveness and trust with God and one another; denial of participation was "spiritual brokenness and separation, isolation from God and the Body of Christ. The act of shunning by the community of believers meant that one was ostracized, not simply avoided but cut off as "dead" socially, professionally, economically, even from spouse and family. To the credit of this congregation, the guidance and leadership of the Session, the Minutes record that prayers were continually offered for those who had been removed from the rolls, that in this life-time they would return to the light. Communication with these persons continued, even after removal from the rolls, and for all whose families requested, their remains were eventually buried from the church by the pastor.

While there were numerous other church disciplinary trials during this era, these were among the longest and most publicized at the time. Considering the number of such experiences, it is a wonder the church survived in any form.

THE TWO "FIRST PRESBYTERIAN" CHURCHES

A different kind of tribulation of the church arose from the "unchristian conduct" of a fist fight in the barn of "Cook and Culver" on the 3rd of May 1838. Afterward, Brother Isaac Smith repented of the unchristian conduct demonstrated by him and Brother John Turner. Brother Isaac Smith appeared before the Session on the 9th day of June 1838 expressing a willingness to make public confession before the church and community. Six weeks after the fight, he made his confession on the 16th of June 1838. The Session repeatedly cited Brother Turner, to appear, to confess and to repent, as well. The bitter feelings engendered, as well as the autocratic inquisitorial exercise of power on the part of the Session, resulted in a division within the church, ultimately causing formation of a second congregation within the same building, name and Pastoral leadership from the 28th day of December 1838 until the 26th day of April 1841. This second church body worshiped God, held meetings and fellowship within the church building, completely separate from their brothers and sisters. According to the Minutes of the church, the membership had elected Brother John Turner to serve as their Moderator. The primary distinctions of the second First Presbyterian congregation was that the governing body while named as Elders, shall not be ordained; also that if a member is to be dealt with for any form of misconduct, said member shall have the privilege if they wish to appeal the decision of the Session to the Presbytery or the congregation. At the final meeting of the second First Presbyterian Church, the Session unanimously resolved that looking at the state of the church in her present form and divisive state, it was necessary to dissolve or to be re-united. The two congregations did re-unite and acted to purge their separate Minutes from the public record as an act of repentance on both parts, for the wounding of the Body of Christ throughout this time.

THE CASE OF CHARLES PARDEE VS. REV. SHELDON HAYNES

In the second fifty years of the first Century of the church, there were relatively few disciplinary cases, probably not because there had not been as many occasions as in previous years, but because the congregation had had enough of such experiences. The case between Mr. Charles Pardee, the Rev. Sheldon Haynes, and the Session, is a prime example why the church had become burdened by the exercise of Church Discipline.

A member of the church, Mr. Charles Pardee bore malice against the pastor, the Rev. Mr. Sheldon Haynes, for possessing a letter of agreement, which both parties had nullified. Due to this malice, the "professor of religion and truth" then sent a letter through the Federal mails to the former church of the Rev. Mr. Haynes in South Arlington, said letter containing money. The letter requested copy of a local newspaper containing libel and editorials of innuendo, or other possible misdeeds of the pastor be sent to First Presbyterian Church of Skaneateles, by which to tarnish his name and reputation. Undaunted, Mr. Pardee attempted to send money through the mail to the newspaper in question, seeking a copy in order to libel the pastor, bearing the church's name as return address. The local postmaster, recognizing that loose currency was included in the letter, returned the letter undelivered to the church, where the letter was presented to the Session and Pastor.

Mr. Pardee then circulated a petition, asking others to sign, in request of dissolving the pastoral relationship on grounds that according to Mr. Pardee, the pastor Rev. Haynes had lied about him (being false witness). Discussion of the conflict first appeared in the Session Minutes of 29 January 1855. For attempting to destroy the peace and unity of the body of Christ, doing harm to God by seeking evil against another in the name of the church, the Session met with Mr. Pardee, attempting to have him put down his complaints in writing that the Session might respond.

19 March 1855 a courtroom style trial began, with the pastor, Rev. Sheldon Haynes acting as Prosecutor, and Mr. Pardee having the counsel of another minister of Presbytery, with the Rev. S.M. Hopkins, DD presiding over the trial as Judge, at the request of the Session acting as Jury. The trial continued daily, beginning at 8am, taking recess at 1pm, and continuing into the evening each day until the decision could be rendered, which was on 06 April 1855. The decision of the Session was that while allegations might be able to be supported on either side, and while the Pastor had exhausted every means of coming to an amiable settlement, because Mr. Pardee was unrelenting in his attacks upon the pastor, and his willingness to destroy the peace and unity of the church, Mr. Pardee should be denied the rights of membership until he had given satisfactory evidence of repentance.

Resolution of this matter was then read to the congregation at the conclusion of the next occurrence of the Lord's Supper. Mr. Pardee appealed this matter to the Presbytery, which upon hearing the testimony and deliberating, commended the Session for their conscientious action and sincere regard for both pastor and member of the church. However, the Presbytery overturned the judgement and required Mr. Pardee be nurtured by the ministry of the church. However, Mr. Pardee absented himself from the church until after the pastor had left this call. 21 September 1855 the pastor resigned. On 09 October, 1855 after several postponements, Mr. Pardee presented the Session a paper which the Session determined constituted a sincere desire to walk together in Christian fellowship.

MORE RECENT HISTORIC CONFLICTS

While Church Discipline can at times appear petty, moralistic and vindictive, there are occasions when discipline not executed can severely harm the little ones, as described by Jesus. In the latter weeks of the Interim Pastorate of the Rev. Dr. Steve Thomas (1994-1996), while finalizing the Call of the next installed pastor, the Session discovered circumstances of a prior pastor's departure 25 years earlier. According to legal affidavits filed, the pastor of the late 1960s had been accused of having violated the trusts and confidence of the ordained ministry in abuse.

The methodology of resolving problems in the church has changed many times from the time of Judas' betrayal and Peter's denial, through the disciplinary trials of the 1800s, to the present day. In 1970, the Church practice, when a pastor was removed by Presbytery Action had been immediate removal from this congregation, without explanation or interaction between the accuser and abuser. While intending to protect the 15 victims from further harm, the victims of the sexual abuse of Rev. Steve Panko had been unable to grieve their violation at the time, or to have acknowledgement from the church. This is a painful part of the recent history of the church. Steve Panko's clouded departure resulted in a gross violation of the most intimate trust, of communion, as well as serious financial debt for the congregation in providing for this man's removal, as well as loss of Capital Fund pledges for the Dobson Hall building program, along with loss of pledges for the annual Operating Budget. What had been the largest and strongest membership in the church's history, suddenly plunged the church into debt and crisis. Due to the careful, prudent fiduciary work of the Session, the church was able to return to a stable fiscal foundation.

Twenty-five years later, when Steve Panko was again making application for another church's pastoral leadership, during a routine reference check, circumstances led back to Skaneateles and re-opened the buried crisis. When confronted with the reality of the sins which occurred in the late 1960s, Mr. Panko avoided responsibility by renouncing the jurisdiction of the Presbyterian Church and abandoned his ordination vows. While those offenses took place during the cultural experimentation of relationships in the late 1960s, Mr. Panko abused his power and authority and the trust of a pastor with adolescent and college-aged children of the church. Interim Pastor Rev. Dr. Steve Thomas and the Session of 1996 worked diligently to excise this cancer, taking great pains to listen to those abused, then prosecute the offender for the dual abuse of violation and betrayal, as well as these offenses having been ignored and disbelieved.

The Roman Catholic Church has appropriately been sued and scandalized for condoning the pedophilia abuses of their priests; but every community of trust is vulnerable to betrayal when a minister with unchecked power, chooses to violate those who trust them, even more when the community condones his/her actions by denial that abuse could have happened. The 13 to 23-year-old, teen-aged and college-aged women whom Steve Panko abused, not only suffered the betrayal of their innocence in the sexual intimacy of this man soliciting their affections, acting in a grossly inappropriate manner for any married middle-aged man; he was their pastor; he represented God, Truth, Trust, Forgiveness, Salvation. This predator, then compounded his sin by denying it had ever happened, at the time and forty years later, hiding behind the power of his role and his being trusted. Those in leadership in the 1960s attempted to seek closure by his immediate removal, which came by paying him severance, and recommending him to other schools and churches, refusing to discuss his abuses or their condoning of this, any further. For four decades, these women tried to be heard, only to have their parents and families, their Sunday School teachers and mentors, their Church and community, and later pastors all deny that what they said was real could have ever happened. How does a victim go to Worship, when it was a trusted minister, an extension of your family, who was responsible for causing you such harm? How do you listen to a sermon? How do you pray to God? How do fulfill your marriage vows, when the one you trusted as intimately and thoroughly as the minister who confirmed you and married you, violated that Sacred trust? How do you fulfill your Ordination vows as an Elder or Deacon, when a minister betrayed his and later renounced his vows? Again, the systemic problem created by abuse, is that because the system seeks to return to homeostasis without first naming and treating the cause of dysfunction, the family-system, each and all the individuals within the system begin to believe that rules and roles and boundaries do not apply to them, and abhorrent behaviors become condoned as normal.

Simultaneous to this 40-year-old abuse finally being prosecuted at the Presbytery-level, the Pastor Nominating Committee chaired by Jack Howard, with Phyllis Clark, Penny Allyn, Gardner McLean, Dave Rossi, Bill McCauley, Peter Swartz, Cynda Penfield, and Michael Capron was interviewing candidates to become the new Installed Pastor in the weeks surrounding Labor Day 1996. As the final candidate, Rev. Lindsey was informed by the Presbytery's Committee on Ministry that should he be elected, his first order of business would be to make certain this scandal was no longer secret from the Session or Congregation, never again forgotten; and second, he would be working to heal the wounds of this long festering cancer to any trust.

THE CO-PASTORATE

During the mid-1980s a creative pattern of leadership suggested for large stable churches, was bringing along a co-pastor throughout the latter part of a pastoral ministry for transition. Rather than the hierarchical system of a Senior and Associate Pastors, this was thought to provide a parity in ministry, during smooth and uninterrupted transition. However, more often than not, this has been an attempt to avoid the critique of an interim examining different ways of doing ministry. These relationships also require the congregation to create a false reality, where two individuals are both in leadership equally, which cannot be maintained for more than six months, which in this case was finally arrested after four years of struggle. A "co-pastorate" is designed to be the means of transition of power, however in this case, there was never any attempt to transition from the former pastor to the new installed pastor having solo authority.

The attempt to create a co-pastorate at Skaneateles First Presbyterian Church between Rev. Dr. Earle Eastman and Rev. George Taylor proved to be problematic. According to Church leadership expert Lyle Schaller, co-pastorates are designed solely to benefit the ministers, not to benefit the church, and can only work when there is a full relationship of trust, commitment and support between both pastors, and between the pastors and the congregation and community; meaning a lack of any conflict, which here at the time was a buried secret. Rev. Dr. Earle Eastman had been installed as the only pastor of this church for nearly twenty years, when the new relationship began. Rev. Eastman was the advocate for having a co-pastorate, who then was responsible for the division of responsibilities, and creating the relationship with the candidate. Rev. Eastman retained full authority and responsibility for the Administration of the church, while Rev. Taylor was given responsibility for creating the Program. The decision to suddenly increase the church's operating budget with the cost of a second ordained pastor placed considerable burden upon the resources of the congregation, as well as expectation solely upon the second pastor to perform to make up the difference. However, Rev. Taylor also had significant personal debt from college and seminary, parenting a young and growing family, and attempting to build a new house in a neighboring township, all of which were problematic in a small community seeking a social relationship with their pastors.

An added difficulty in this circumstance was that Rev. Dr. Eastman as the installed pastor, occupied the historic manse overlooking the church and Village and Lake, from atop the prestigious Academy Street, while Rev. Taylor chose to purchase land and build a home outside the Village and Township of Skaneateles in the Town of Sennett. This became a financial burden to Rev. Taylor, while the economic benefits of home ownership became something coveted by Rev. Dr. Eastman. Most significant of all, the relationship between these two personalities was an inability to represent trust as pastors in each other to the church. Ultimately, both ministers wanted the authority of being The Pastor, without having to share power with another, while neither desired all the responsibilities that came with this church. This is a prime example of individuals within the system believing that rules and roles and boundaries do not apply to them, and abhorrent behaviors being condoned as normal.

The congregation fractioned between supporters of one over the other. Once again, the identity of two congregations, worshiping in spite of the other, within one church building became a reality. Alban Institute: Conflict Management Specialists were hired to guide the congregation through the many overlapping layers of conflict. However, on the very day their final report and recommendations were to be presented to Session and Presbytery representatives for action, Rev. Dr. Eastman undercut the Consultants' report by tendering his resignation, announcing that he would live out his days in the town of Skaneateles.

In the years following which, in the absence of the co-pastors, the Session has been challenged with far greater responsibility for transparency of decision-making. The goal of having the Session own decisions, rather than having pastors with unquestioned authority, has been intentional to create greater trust and accountability. No longer are there decisions made behind closed doors. There are clear and objective policies and guidelines for everything to be open and available for the congregation to understand and comment upon. There have been circumstances regarding the retirement of a long-term pastor, and the functioning of the co-pastorate, as well as the pastoral abuses and misconduct of the late 1960s, and even the critical need for building renovations, which became un-necessarily problematic and central to this dysfunction was the congregation's history of secret conflict.

When the parts of the body of Christ demonize one another, when the church is consistently divided in the same ways among the same persons regardless of issue, that conflict intensifies from being issue-based to becoming systemic. The work of rebuilding the church's foundations, lifting and stabilizing the Sanctuary foundations, changing the aisles of worship, replacing lighting and windows in Dobson Hall to let the light in, all have been parabolic of the pastoral ministry in this era, re-establishing that Jesus Christ is our sure foundation. Hyperbolic in this, is that the climax of the co-pastorate was celebration of the Centennial Anniversary of the Sanctuary, for which one of the members re-wrote the words of the hymn "Christ is Made the Sure Foundation."

MEMBERSHIP STATISTICS

While statistics can be dry and boring and can often be used by Pastors to make arbitrary comparisons of size, without accounting for the standards of the times, numbers do provide a witness to transitions distinct from all other accounts.

On 20 July 1801, The First Presbyterian Church of Skaneateles was organized, having 15 (fifteen) members.

From the date of organization until Mr. Swift's pastorate ended (less than two years 1811-1813) the records account for 70 additional persons having been added to the membership.

During Benjamin Rice's pastorate of 4 years (1813-1817), there were 62 additions.

During Rev. B.B. Stockton's four-year pastorate (1818-1822) there were 87 additions.

During Rev. Cowan's pastorate of six years (1822-1828, there were 50 additions.

During Rev. Samuel Brace's pastorate of 15 years (1828-1843) there were 249 additions.

During Rev. Samuel Bush's pastorate of seven years (1844-1851) there were 40 additions.

During Rev. Sheldon Haynes' four-year pastorate (1851-1855) there were 77 additions.
During Rev. W.B. Daba's pastorate of two years (1856-1858) there were 27 additions.

During Rev. A. Mandell's two-year pastorate (1859-1861) there were 20 additions.

During Rev. M. N. Preston's 22-year pastorate (1862-1884) there were 385 additions.

During Rev. E. G. Cheeseman's 9 months (1885-6) there were 38 additions.

During Rev. O. L. White's pastorate of 17 years (1887-1904) there were 274 additions.

During the Stated Supply of Rev. E.J. Humeston (1904-1906) there were 30 additions.

During the 5-year pastorate of Rev. John A. Rodger (1907-1912) there were 89 additions.

During the seven-year pastorate of Rev. Alfred Vail (1912-1919) there were 81 additions,
 as the world experienced and recovered from the first of the wars to end all wars.

During the thirteen-year pastorate of Rev. FC Scorge (1920-1932) the United States experienced the Stock Market Crash and the church experienced 132 additions.

During Rev. Albert C. Fulton's five-year pastorate (1933-1938) 75 members joined.

During Rev. John Dobson's 28-year pastorate (1938-1966) there were 429 new members.

During Rev. Steve Panko's four years (1966-1970), there were 236 additions.
During Interim Pastor Rev. Steve Palmer's year, there were 9 new members.

During Rev. Dr. Earle Eastman's 19-year pastorate (1971-1989) and four-year co-pastorate there were 475 additions. Thirty of these were added during the co-pastorate with Rev. George Taylor (1989-1994). Yet, Net Membership remained static 1972-1994.

During the Interim Pastorate of Rev. Dr. Steve Thomas (1994-1996) there were 46 added.

During the pastorate of The Rev. Dr. Craig J. Lindsey (1996-Present) there have been 493 new members, 275 baptisms, and 322 weddings. 27 of these new members joined during the years with Associate Pastor Rev. Mario Bolivar.

215 Year History of Net Communicant Membership 1801-2016 by 5 Year Increments

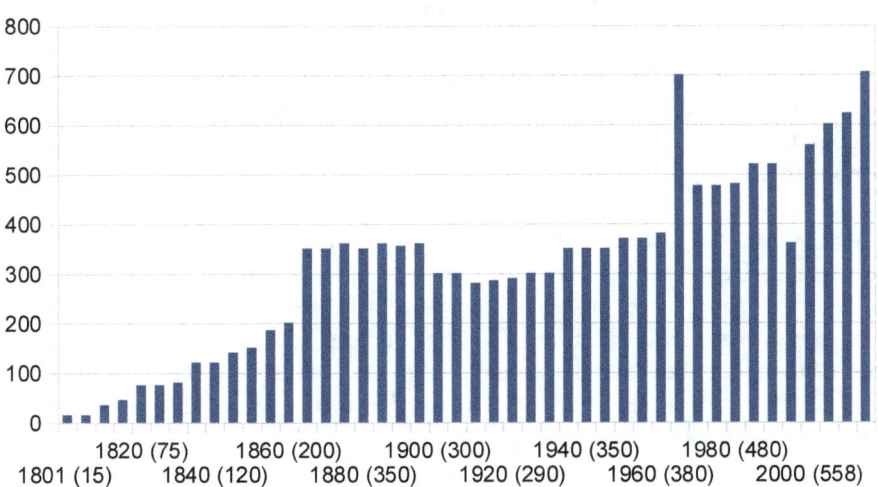

Therefore, in our first century, the records show there had been 1,507 new members to this church. In the second hundred years, an additional 2,131 members received, and already in our third century there have been 275. A total of 3,893 souls have joined the communion of this body. The membership of the Religious Society began with 15 believers, 7 men and 8 women in 1801. From those first meetings until 1868, the total active communicant membership on the rolls of the church never surpassed 136 adults. Between 1868 and 1901 the church is reported as having held three Revival meetings, in 1869, 1873 and 1890, consistent with the Great Awakening Movement of Jonathan Edwards and the Second Great Awakening of the "burned-over district". Active membership of the church increased two and a half times in those thirty years, to a total of 346 adults by 1901. The membership remained between 345 and 400 persons until 1954. From 1954 until 1960 the congregation consistently grew with the American Baby-boom to a maximum of 541.

The pastorate of Steve Panko was extremely charismatic, and between 1966 and 1970, the church's membership swelled to in excess of 700 persons. However, this brief ministry ended abruptly, and whether in anger over what the pastor had done, or allegiance to him, that year the church lost 224 members returning to 476. Following the conflicts of the co-pastorate the membership was 480. While Session has repeatedly cleaned the Rolls, membership in 2016 is again 703 adult members. Current circumstance also confuses membership numbers, as New York State taxes "residents" at 33% where Florida taxes residents at 0% for Income tax. One of the ways in which New York State has "proven" membership has been church membership, forcing those who contribute to this church and have been "members" for generations to transfer their membership to Florida churches while continuing to claim this as "their church." This practice has led the current pastor to question the State's violation of the United States Constitution in telling citizens where they can and cannot worship God. This could account for another 150 persons.

There had been 31 Elders in the first century of the church, 1801-1900. Elder J. Augustus Edwards died 29 March 1894 who for nearly half a century had held the ordained office of elder. Chauncy Clark was recognized in 1943 for having completed four decades of service of Session. Until 1852, both elders and deacons were ordained and installed in service without limit. Beginning in 1852, the term of these offices was fixed at three years with one-third the officers rotating in and out every year.

In the first century, there were sixteen ordained deacons. Deacon William E. Clark belonged to a famous family of church officers. His grandfather and father had been deacons in this church before him; his great-grandfather and great-great-grandfather had been deacons in a Presbyterian church in Massachusetts, making five consecutive generations prior to 1900 ordained as Deacons of the church. Mr. William Clark also had a son, but he broke the family tradition by becoming an Elder in the Presbyterian Church in Dakota, as well as a grandson and great-grandson who were recognized as leaders in that church.

First Presbyterian Church also had a Board of Trustees from 1891 until 1961. The Centennial account of Rev. O.L. White records the indebtedness of the church to this Board.

"In the erecting of this building, and the liquidating of all indebtedness thereon, in looking after and preserving our imperiled legacies, and in meeting promptly the current expenses, the Trustees have done much hard work faithfully. To them is due largely the degree of prosperity which the church enjoys. The 1901 Board of Trustees was composed of: Phillip Allen, Joseph Shotwell, Professor H.F. Miner, George M. Talcott, William G. Stuart and Edward C. Miller."

These are also among the most prominent names in the heritage of the Village of Skaneateles.

SPECIALIZED MINISTRIES

The church is a people of God meeting to offer praise to God in thanksgiving. The church in North America has also become a building, or series of buildings, used for worship and community service. The church is the accumulation of all its work in education, music and choirs, missions, fellowship, investments and endowments.

THE SABBATH SCHOOL

Among the various organizations within the church, there comes first the Sabbath School. This was originally organized during the pastorate of Rev. B B John Stockton in 1821. Building upon the earlier mission of the Religious Society, the purposes of the first Sunday School were not so much to teach the Bible and religion, as to develop rudimentary knowledge of the alphabet and reading. However, using the Bible as the primary teaching aid, in replacement of a McGuffy Reader the Sunday School quickly grew into a decisively religious school, and ever since has been the fruitful nursery of the church. During the late 1800s, four different adult Bible study groups met simultaneously in the Sanctuary, segregated as to whether men or women, and studying the Old or New Testaments.

When the new Sanctuary was dedicated in 1892, the room immediately outside the Sanctuary (now part of the Sims Room) had been the Primary aged classroom. Two massive pocket doors were drawn across this room, where stantion support poles now stand. In the 1928 Renovations prompted by Miss Allen, this "classroom" became the church kitchen, as a wall was built where the pocket-doors had been, with a pass-through window and plumbed in indoor sink with hot and cold running water. The Beginners and Primary classes met upstairs in the Kellogg Room from this time until the 1950s; with those in the 3rd grade and younger meeting during worship, and those in 4th grade and older meeting after worship. When the Cellar of the Sanctuary had been dug out in 1957, this added whole new spaces for the burgeoning Sunday School. Graded curriculum with separate classes did not begin until 1915.

From 1900 until the early 1960s the church had Sunday School Superintendents. Mrs. Danser, Wesley Weeks and Willis Cleveland provided these gifts for a decade each 1900 – 1930. Irene Dodd, Kitty Donaldson, Marian Arnold rotated being Superintendent in the 1940s. Olive Fisher and Chuck Evans administered the Sunday School throughout the 1950s, and Jack Howard in the 1960s.

April 26, 1964 a Special meeting of the Session was held for the purpose of creating a Part-Time position of Director of Christian Education. A year-long search was held, and Elizabeth Denier was hired 27 September 1965. Betty (Mailanetti) Woolston replaced Elizabeth Denier 1966-1968. In 1968 Assistant Pastor David Becker was Called as a second minister on staff with responsibilities for Christian Education. Nancy Bethel was hired as Rev. Becker's Administrative Assistant in 1969. Following Rev. Becker's term, Doris Kohlligian served as Part-Time Director of Christian Education from 01 August 1970 until 1974. In 1974, Mrs. Marilyn Shinaman was hired part-time and the following year, 1975, increased to full-time Director of Christian Education.

However, this created its own problems, in that Full-Time Christian Educators were per denominational standards required to receive employment benefits "like" pastors. In the course of her own journey of faith, the church sponsored Marilyn Shinaman's continuing education by her attending Seminary for Certification as a Christian Educator. Difficulty arose when she continued eventually completing all course-work for graduation with a Masters in Divinity degree without having ever been Under Care of Session or Presbytery. At which point, she sought Ordination and Installation as a Minister of Word and Sacrament, while Dr. Eastman had wanted a different candidate to serve as his Associate Pastor. Mrs. Shinaman celebrated the Presbytery's Ordination of her here at Skaneateles, never serving here as a pastor here, but at the Aurora and Scippioville Churches.

Margy Lee and Kathy Hilliard each served as part-time Christian Education Assistants from 1995-1999. While it would be impossible to name all those who have faithfully given of their time and faith as teachers, three shining stars stand out: Martha Cross, Penny Allyn and Dawn Allyn each provided over three decades of service.

In 1999, Rev. Lindsey came to Session stating the need for an Associate Pastor. The Session investigated the purposes and priorities of Christian Education within the total overall ministry of the church, and because of recent pain over the Co-Pastorate instead resolved to hire and professionally train a "Certified Christian Education Director." The Session also clarified a need to uphold a Personnel Policy to hire for employment only non-members of the church for paid staff positions. Lynda Fauler was hired 01/01/2000 to serve 30 hours per week as Director of Christian Education. What Lynda Fauler had not made known to the church or pastor, was that in the same way as Marilyn Shinaman, Lynda Fauler had previously taken all necessary coursework to be Certified as a Christian Educator, without ever having had Presbytery Care or Direction, so upon hire she quickly progressed through her Certification process with required salary increases, without the Pastor, Church or Presbytery being able to be part of her education, supervision or application of training. A piece of this missing supervision related to boundaries, as Lynda often wanted to preach and visit parishioners, as if a pastor. Lynda Fauler retired from this position in 2010. Now ten years later, the Session again had come to a time of questioning the professional training of this position. For a year, the church had no staff person in this position. In June 2011, the Session directed the Pastor to find the most qualified person possible to serve in a Part-time temporary capacity, not only in Christian Education but Spiritual Direction.

During the 2010-11 Academic year without a designated Christian Educator, the Session (with prior knowledge of Committee On Ministry and congregation) engaged in a thorough Mission Study, bringing pieces of the Mission Study to the congregation for feedback, recommending in the Fall of 2011 that the congregation consider Calling an Associate Pastor. The congregation reacted quite strongly against this for three stated reasons:

> 1. The Call process can often take at least 12 months
> 2. Once Installed, an Associate Pastor cannot be removed except by Presbytery
> 3. The relationship between Pastors must be carefully developed and shared.

The Session then discussed alternatives, recognizing that the Session does have authority to hire employees and could create a Parish Associate employment position. Different from a Christian Educator, a Parish Associate must be an Ordained Minister. Different from an Associate Pastor, a Parish Associate is not Installed in a Call by the Congregation and Presbytery, but is directly accountable as an employee to the Session and Senior Pastor. As such, a Parish Associate could be hired without a lengthy Search/Call process, would have specific responsibilities, and whenever the Senior Pastor resigned the Parish Associate position would automatically be terminated without prejudice. To the Session this addressed each of the congregation's concerns.

The Rev. Debra Thomas had been a Spanish Teacher in the Liverpool School System, who then went to Seminary and was Under Care of Presbytery seeking Ordination as a Minister. Rev. Thomas was ordained in 2000 and served a decade as a solo pastor in the Weedsport Church within the Presbytery. She decided to take time to reframe her ministry and resigned from that Call. Rev. Lindsey invited her to consider the opportunity of being Parish Associate, which might grow into something more and different.

The Session set about hiring Rev. Debra Thomas to serve as full-time Parish Associate beginning 01 April 2012 with responsibility for Spiritual Nurture. Specifically, she would not have regular responsibility for Preaching or Worship leadership, or Session Administration, or for Pastoral Care. In this way, the church was able to hire the skills of a creative, ordained leader to begin immediately; Rev. Thomas was able to have a position that used the skills and creativity she wanted to share, without all the demands of a solo pastoral Call, and both knew one another already. Unfortunately, within the year, for her own family reasons, Rev. Thomas resigned.

Undiagnosed at the time, a new conflict had been fostered within the Music staff. The Organist at the time had recommended the hiring of her spouse as Choral Director. Both had been trained and experienced College Professors. Universities are often described as being like Middle-ages Fiefdoms, with the President as King or Queen, Department Heads as contesting Barons. This duo set about creating their own power and cadres, which while the quality of music performed became Concert level, personal relationships eroded. During this time, the Parish Associate, installation of a Restroom in the Narthex, and other actions of the Session and Pastor's leadership all were challenged. The Organist had numerous personal demands, of prohibiting anyone the use of the Northeast door to the Sanctuary, building a wall around the Organ console so she could not be seen, refusing to play piano to accompany the Children's Choir or soloists, etc. Once this husband-wife duo was fired by the Session through the Pastor, the church immediately returned to calm communion.

Again, the Session came to the congregation, but now instead of the Pastor urging this, the impetus for an Associate Pastor came directly from the Session members. On the basis of the Session members' own professions of commitment, the Congregation held a Special Congregational Meeting to act to petition the Presbytery of Cayuga Syracuse for the definition of Call of this congregation to be changed from Solo Pastor, to a Senior Pastor (Rev. Lindsey) and an un-named Associate Pastor. The Associate Pastor to function as a fully installed pastor of the Church, but with specific responsibilities for Technology, Christian Education and Youth, and for extending the Ministry of the Church to long-distance members who had been married here, presented children for Baptism but only worship occasionally each year due to living out of the area. An Associate Pastor Nominating Committee was elected including: Doug Rutan, Todd Marshall, Claudia Lambdin, Ginny Fennessy and Kathleen Witter. The Session having already researched and written the Mission Study, the search began immediately and within four months the APNC recommended we Ordain and Install the Mario Bolivar as our Associate Pastor. Being in such a homogeneously Caucasian community the congregation had not intentionally sought to have a Hispanic, Latin, Immigrant Pastor; but recognizing him to be the best qualified candidate, recommended by the process, the Church saw extending this Call as expanding the appeal of the Church for the 21st Century. Rev. Mario Bolivar was Ordained and Installed September 2014.

THE MINISTRY OF MUSIC

As far back as anyone can find, members of this church have loved to sing. Throughout the Religious Revival days of the 1800s, the church sang a wide range of Gospel hymns. From the early 1900s until after WWII the church employed soloists, first for solo work, later as support and guide for each section of the choir. The one stipulation of the Session during this era (other than the musical ability of the soloist) was that no paid soloist could be the chairperson of the Worship and Music Committee. Currently, the church enjoys the great benefit of having many talented, enthusiastic choirs and ensembles, without paid soloists.

Bunt Osborne began as Organist in 1964, filling in when his aunt went to the hospital with Heart condition. Mr. Osborne continued in this capacity for another 40 years. Bunt had been trained as an Organist, but professionally had always been a farmer. At age 84, having played for forty years, Bunt retired as Organist, and the Worship Committee had his shoes "bronzed." Bunt's mother (Gertrude Osborne) had been Director of Music during the 1940-1970s. When she was forced to retire, Maureen McCauley became Director of Music. Maureen also created the Masterworks Chorale which rehearsed at the Skaneateles Presbyterian Church. Quite abruptly in the 1980s, Ms. McCauley resigned to tour Europe investigating Chorale programs like Masterworks Chorale. After an extended period without a designated Choral Director, the Session hired Tom Baker. Mr. Baker had a Masters in Piano Performance from Crane Music School, but no experience or training in conducting. Passive Aggressive problems between Bunt and Tom began early in the relationship. At one point in the 1980s, the Session appointed an Investigative Committee chaired by Jack Howard. The

Committee recommended to Session both be fired, but Rev. Eastman fearing how this would be accepted by the congregation, over-ruled this Investigative Committee Recommendation to recommend that Tom be made "Director of Music" in addition to being Chancel Choir Director. The Director of Music title came with additional responsibilities for accountability and compensation. However, the relationship between the two was always a matter of toleration and avoidance. Bunt was succeeded by Janet Correl, then by Karen Hindenlang.

Ms. Hindenlang was a far superior musician than the church had previously enjoyed, but she had a high need for control. Two years after Ms. Hindenlang began, Tom Baker retired. Several months later, the volunteer Director of Choirs for Children also resigned. While advertising for the Chancel Choir Director, the pastor contacted the Syracuse Children's Chorus for recommendations for a Children's Choir Director, and the Director of the Chorus responded that she was seeking an additional responsibility with a Church. Stephanie Mowery, a Westminster Choir College Graduate, with extensive experience began as Director of Children's Choirs 2011, and instantly expanded from one choir to multiple ensembles of children. A thorough search was done for a new Chancel Choral Director, however all of the candidates except one, were like Tom Baker trained as a performance artist not a conductor, and that one candidate was Karen Hindenlang's husband, Crawford Thoburn. Dr. Thoburn had been Head of the Music Department at Wells College and was a recognized composer. The music performed by the Chancel Choir improved dramatically, but two problems arose. The Choir members were yelled at by the Director, and members of the Choir began to name the distinction between Concert performance and Worship of God. Both Ms. Hindenlang and Dr. Thoburn were warned of the need for fellowship over quality of musical performance. The persons making complaints were encouraged to speak directly with the staff, not triangulating the pastor or Session. Ultimately, when Annual Evaluations were done, the pastor informed both that they were being let go.

Church members and in particular members of the Choir were concerned how we could replace such qualified musicians. By the grace of God, one of the colleagues whom Ms. Hindenlang contacted regarding her departure was Doris Hill. Ms. Hill had been Senior Organist at Second Presbyterian Church in Bloomington, Illinois a very large congregation with exceptional music program. She had recently retired, to spend time near their son who lived in Skaneateles, before returning to Bloomington for their latter days. Doris Hill contacted the pastor to volunteer that she could provide the church with a year of performance as Organist. The pastor approached Stephanie Mowery to conduct the Choir for the remainder of the school year, she did, then applied to be considered for Director of all Vocal Choirs. Rather than a professorial role, Ms. Mowery's style was to solicit involvement and ask for participation. Rather than the Director, or a few voices dominating the choir, the entire choir found its faith, voice and a heart for singing.

In early 2016 Stephanie Mowery elected to leave Central New York to care for her parents in Oregon. Prior to her departure, the pastor sought out Sue Grady who was a long-time member of the congregation, the Hand-Bell Choir Director and a Second-Grade teacher. Mrs. Grady was invited, because she had no aspirations to be considered as Chancel Choir Director, because she knew the persons and repertoire involved, to consider serving as Interim Director through the School year. She accepted and provided exceptional leadership and a buffer after the Choir's relationship with Ms. Mowery before introduction of a new Chancel Choir Director.

A Nation-wide search was held for the Choral Director position, advertising among Teachers, Musicians, Choral Directors and Organists. While the Session received a number of fine candidates, one stood out for their faith as well as their education and experience. Ironically, he was the grandson of Gertude Osborne, and nephew of Bunt Osborne, named Brian Ackles.

THE MARGARET SPITZER ENDOWMENT

Margaret Spitzer had been a life-long member of this congregation and a local music teacher, who died in 1998. Her sons were world re-known eye surgeons. Meeting with Mrs. Spitzer's family following her death, they described desire to create an endowment in her honor. Rev. Lindsey recommended that because of Margaret's love of music, that this endowment be invested and re-invested, that periodically the growth and interest would be used to commission a new piece of music for the First Presbyterian Church, which would be published with that attribute. Thus, far three pieces, one for Chancel Choir, one for Organ and one for Handbells, have been published and enjoyed by the congregation.

THE CROSSMAN/SODERBERG SCHOLARSHIP

Margaret (Margie) Crossman and Mary Soderberg had been highly educated women of faith, and long-time members of First Presbyterian Church. Margie Crossman left an endowment to the church for the creation of a Scholarship fund to be used annually to support members of the Church seeking further education. When Mary Soderberg died, her family re-invested in this scholarship to allow more students to continue to apply.

THE PRESBYTERIAN WOMEN'S ASSOCIATION AND CIRCLES

In 1856, The Women's Missionary Society was organized "to help those less fortunate". Records describe that women knit rolled bandages, packed canned goods for soldiers in wartime, and prayed together. During "Prohibition," a Ladies' Aid Society was formed "to help those in need, to pray for and to encourage them." The Women's Missionary Society and The Ladies' Aid Society merged into the Presbyterian Women's Association and Circles in 1941. In the days of Prohibition, a "Happy Hour Club" was created of Church Women gathering for fellowship.

Throughout the years, the women of the church have served as Elders and Deacons, as well as funding the sending of youth to camp, funding the work of mission, designing curtains and sewing choir robes. While permitted by the Constitution of the Presbyterian Church since 1927, the first woman Elder was elected and ordained in this congregation in 1950, the first woman Deacon in 1967. For many years, Elizabeth and Marshall Larabee, owners of The T.C. Timber Wooden Toy Train Company brought their company's imperfect toys to our church's cellar, where volunteers "reconciled the imperfections" remaking these misfit toys for donation to missions around the world. The Women's Association has provided monthly meetings for Bible Study, Fellowship and Mission.

THE PRESBYTERIAN MEN

The Presbyterian Men's group provides monthly breakfast programs for the church, adding to the congregation's fellowship, education and a feeding of the flock. Each Spring, the men of the church host an adult picnic. In addition, the men of the church do great good work, volunteering behind the scenes of church and community.

THE MINISTRY TO COMMUNITY YOUTH

A Young People's Society was started in 1875, eventually organized under the Christian Endeavors constitution. Our congregation has consistently attempted to minister "to bands (gangs) of boys and girls described to be of more or less evanescent character." In the 1960s our church weekly sponsored community dances, opening up Dobson Hall for local disc jockeys and bands to play. So many young people attended these dances that the local police volunteered an officer to serve as chaperone.

THE DUK LOST BOYS' SUDANESE CLINIC and THE JOHN DAU FOUNDATION

In July of 2001, four Refugees were sponsored by the 1st Presbyterian Church of Skaneateles, New York, USA. As children, their village of Duk Payuel in what was then southern Sudan, had been burned by troops. These children walked across Sudan to Ethiopia, where they lived in a refugee camp for 8 years. When Ethiopia was drawn into civil war, they were walked at gunpoint back to Sudan, where they walked to the Kakuma Refugee Camp in Kenya. After another 10 years in refugee camps, they came to Central New York. Their story of identity and survival is chronicled in the Sundance Film Festival award-winning film *God Grew Tired of Us*.

A simple idea changed this entire program into relationships of ministry. A clipboard was passed during worship, inviting those willing to drive to East Syracuse and back on Sunday mornings to bring the Sudanese to worship. Sit with them in worship, then bring them into your home, sharing the Sabbath meal with them, and spending time together, before driving them back to their apartment in Syracuse. Total cost per family 27 miles times 4 trips, plus lunch, and one day of your life. What this accomplished was for each of the refugees to come to know the Skaneateles Presbyterians personally, by worshiping God together, sharing time and breaking bread together, as well as making a simple and personal sacrifice. In our years together, John Dau graduated from Syracuse University Maxwell School; Santino Arak graduated from University of NY at Buffalo in Banking; Andrew Ruach married and had two children while he and his bride went to school; Andrew Majok graduated Suma Cum Laude from LeMoyne University in Biology, he was the first Sudanese to enlist in the United States Military and is serving as the Executive Officer of the Army Base at Utica, NY.

In September 2004, one of these refugees, John Dau, attended a Sudanese Lost Boys' Convention, where they discussed plans to alleviate human suffering in southern Sudan. By November, John Dau was gathering a small group from First Presbyterian Church to help establish a Primary Health Care Clinic in southern Sudan for a cost of $30,000. The first question broached was whether to build a clinic at all—after all, this had been a nomadic culture, and in a war-zone a building might be a target. However, John Dau described the need to demonstrate permanence of health care, and to provide a location people would seek as they returned from refugee camps and the bush to rebuild the country. The second question, was whether we could accomplish this? On February 14, 2005, this group of Americans met with David Bowman, a retired Dentist and sponsor of refugees in Michigan, about how to proceed. Dr. Bowman described that nothing could happen unless someone physically went to Sudan to build trust. Encountering the first dead-end, the pastor Rev. Dr. Craig Lindsey volunteered to go to Sudan for two weeks, to develop relationships of trust, making as many linkages as possible. This became the paradigm of our activity, which later became the John Dau Foundation: every time a dead-end was met, we volunteered ourselves and our skills to make a difference, regardless of risk.

Immediately we began making contacts with members of the new and fledgling Ministry of Health, leaders in the SPLA/SPLM, as well as those of the Government of Sudan, the Presbyterian, Anglican and Catholic Churches, to try to develop partnerships. Six weeks later, April 1st, 2005, Rev. Lindsey flew to Kenya, there to charter a plane to Duk County, Jonglei State, southern Sudan. At every juncture, those who were to accompany him did not show up, and new relationships had to be forged. There were no stores or banks, so he carried $10,000 in $100 bills hidden on his body, this coming from wedding services and donations of parishioners. Arriving in Sudan, the temperature exceeded 120 degrees. Rev. Lindsey began by re-uniting Sudanese with photos and letters from their children. Each knew their families dead for 20 years, now brought back to life.

He shared John Dau's plan to build a Clinic. Village leaders shared stories on how 8 out of 10 children routinely died before age five years, from preventable diseases. They said half of the women died from complications in labor and delivery, with less than 1 in 10 delivering with a skilled midwife. This is a brutal, undeveloped climate, which due to disease, wound infection, a lack of water or electricity, extreme poverty and war, caused people to die. The leaders showed an unfinished building, that had never had water, or power, medicines or staff. They shared need for a Hospital, supported by clinics and smaller health units, all connected by transportation. On behalf of the Foundation, Rev. Lindsey pledged: "We can build one Primary Health Care Clinic. It is better to have this done well, than to attempt to do everything and fail."

Chuie Deng Leek, Paramount Chief of the region, described "What the Reverend offered was a great thing, that if they would do this, Rev. Lindsey and his friends would live a long life. But that the Sudanese had been lied to many times, and if he were not telling the truth of his convictions he would die a miserable and painful death." The following morning he awoke with a high fever and severe loss of fluids from heat prostration. Undaunted, he led worship for 3,000 then met with the priests and pastors of all the surrounding villages to provide them with pastoral care. In the next week, despite being critically ill, we grew to know and trust one another, shared meals at table together, prayed and ministered to the needs of the people, and selected a site for where the clinic would be. For four months every year this region receives as much as 14 inches of rain per day, during which flooding occurs to a depth of one meter of standing water. For the other eight months of the year, temperatures exceed 110 degrees and all water dries up. This is a polygamous dowry culture, so cattle roam defecating everywhere, resulting in insect born diseases. Returning to Kenya, Lindsey made additional contacts, discerning that the cost of construction would be at least $300,000 instead of $30,000 as originally thought.

Rev. Lindsey returned to Syracuse, New York in mid-April 2005 and the American Advisors began a 501(c)3 as the American Care for Sudan Foundation, aimed at establishing the Duk Lost Boys Clinic (later renamed the John Dau Foundation), developed By-Laws, and registered with the Government of Southern Sudan—this was all very complicated because of U.N. sanctions against Sudan, even though this work was with the oppressed in South Sudan. None of the volunteers, including John Dau, had experience with such a project as developing health care in South Sudan, especially to the level of a facility that could serve the entire region and provide emergency obstetrics and neonatal care. We partnered with a non-profit organization specializing in engineering, Tech-Serv International, which constructed a steel-skinned building to cover a concrete slab and block wall to serve as the Clinic, while the Foundation members began fundraising. John Dau traveled the U.S., and the world, speaking on humanitarian issues and the situation in Sudan—his growing popularity raising funds for this and other Lost Boy projects.

By September 2005, two cargo containers were loaded with building materials and tools, as well as donated medical and laboratory equipment for starting a clinic. These two cargo containers were transported from Arkansas to Mombasa, Kenya, where they were to be loaded onto two semi-trailers, driven across the open savannah to Duk County, though no roads existed. Within days of the containers arriving in Kenya, word was received one container had been hi-jacked to Uganda. The second container seemed to disappear completely. In December 2005, John Dau returned to South Sudan for the first time. He explored alternative routes and determined that the initial means, while exploratory, had been the most secure and most economical of traveling to Duk County. He verified the relationship between the Village and Foundation, and formalized the location for the clinic as previously chosen.

As weeks passed, volunteers Don Cross, Mark DeWitt and Ted Kinder determined that whether materials arrived or not, they had a limited window for construction before rains arrived. On February 14, 2006, they left Syracuse in a snowstorm, arriving in Sudan in 110-degree heat. Days were spent determining the final location of the building, burning the 8-foot high grass from the area, laying out level lines, and determining that the only existent fresh water well in the area actually had gone dry. The third night they were in Duk, Don heard a rustling coming toward them through the tall grass. Following GPS, without roads, with no explanation of the container being hi-jacked, both containers drove to the exact location. Forty-eight hours later, the contractors had wired together electrical panels and made repairs to the generator due to damage caused in shipping. The youngest children in the village were called forward to flip a toggle switch, providing the first electric power and light to the clinic location, then to the village. That evening, the contractors went to a marriage of the local chief and happened to meet a well driller from Texas, who at the sponsorship of his church was driving across southern Sudan digging wells. The following morning, the well drilling rig was set up at the clinic site, and by 3pm a fresh well had been dug and submersed pump lowered providing pressurized fresh water.

Dealing with extreme heat, scorpions, black mamba and cobra snakes, rancid food and unskilled laborers, Don, Ted and Mark were able to pour concrete footers and bolt together the steel framing for the building and roof. When Ted and Mark left to return home, a neighboring tribe attacked the village compound to steal their prized cattle. Seven people were killed and many others wounded. Don Cross acted as an emergency medic, applying a tourniquet to a man's femoral artery. Throughout these weeks, international agencies and government aid workers would drive to the clinic site to see first-hand what they were doing. The professionals were surveying costs and verifying need, while our volunteer contractors and Foundation had created an innovative design, by each person donating their time and skills. When Don Cross left, Christian Missionary contractors arrived to continue the work. These contractors turned out to be quite mercenary and disreputable. Chuck Williams, a 77-year-old educator from Skaneateles, NY who happened to write his senior college thesis on the "Tensile Strength of Concrete", volunteered to head-up the next team of volunteer contractors. Following Chuck Williams' two weeks, Don Cross and Mark DeWitt returned for an additional two weeks to finish construction. On May 1, 2006, the contractors left and medical staff arrived. In a matter of 30 days, the Clinic had gone from an empty land to treating patients. From that day until the present, the Duk Clinic of the John Dau Foundation has been in continuous service. The initial staff of a physician assistant, laboratory technician, pharmacist, and nurse, has expanded to include two clinicians, three nurses, two midwives, a pharmacist, two laboratory staff, an HIV counselor, nutritionist, and outreach coordinator.

The Clinic has hosted a number of visiting medical staff. One American doctor's assessment while visiting in 2008 was: "Empires and Kings have built palaces and sanctuaries, but a small group of people spun off as a mission of a church in Upstate New York have given their fortunes, their time and expertise to alleviate human suffering and make a long-term impact on the well-being of people, they will never meet or know."

Dr. David Reed and Dr. Barbara Connor of Syracuse, NY volunteered their time and services at the clinic for several weeks in March 2007 establishing administrative protocols, improving medical services and developing capacity. With their guidance, the clinic began the region's first Tuberculosis testing and treatment program. In the past several years, the clinic developed the region's first HIV and Nutrition programs, led by local South Sudanese trained by our Foundation. In 2009, the Foundation received donation of a solar-powered refrigeration system to serve as a cold chain. A cold-chain is necessary to ensure that vaccines, certain medicines, laboratory supplies, and donated blood remain at a consistent temperature. With this, the Clinic launched the county's first reliable vaccination program.

The Foundation has partnered with: International Relief and Development (IRD), Interchurch Medical Assistance, Heart2Heart, UNICEF, the World Food Programme, UNDP, Samaritan's Purse, Norwegian Peoples' AID, Polish Humanitarian Action, and the new Government of South Sudan. With support of these partners, a new in-patient ward, a maternity ward, and a sterile suite for limited surgery were all constructed and furnished in the past six months. The Ministry of Health has promised, as it builds its capacity, to provide medicines and salaries to ensure the clinic, which the Ministry has now deemed "an example for the entire country," can continue.

Volunteers have returned annually, using their vacations from professional employment to accomplish goals of development at the Clinic. In 2011, an experienced LPN, with a specialty in wound care, taught the Clinic's nursing staff about proper wound care. December 2012, John Dau, Dr. David Reed, Dr. Barbara Connor led a volunteer team of world-renowned eye surgeons to the Clinic, who provided over 200 cataracts and 100 trachoma surgeries in just five days, beginning an annual program of restoring sight to the blind. In February 2012, two construction volunteers began construction of a nutrition center, including a solar power system.

Through the work of the John Dau Foundation, the Duk Lost Boys' Clinic became one of the few full-fledged Basic Emergency Obstetrics and Neo-Natal Care Primary Health Care Centers in the new Republic of South Sudan. 2007-2012, the clinic provided over:

- 170,000 patients with medical care,
- 500 women receive first-time prenatal care,
- 2,000 children with their final dose of DPT vaccination,
- 15,000 school children with deworming,
- 40 people successfully treated for tuberculosis,
- 500 people, over 170 of them mothers, with counseling and testing for HIV/AIDs,
- 1,000 people with community public health awareness education,
- 25 traditional birth attendants with 80 hours of training,
- Support of 5 Primary Health Care Units as satellite screening outposts of the clinic
- 4 County Health Dept. staff have received training in disease surveillance and reporting

In addition, the Clinic has created a reliable satellite Internet service for communication, and an SUV for use as an ambulance as well as for outreach campaigns.

Since we began in 2005, the John Dau Foundation has raised and spent between $300,000 and $2,000,000 per year, all from donations and grants. Up until 2009, all administrative services, costs and labor for the Foundation were provided as a mission of the First Presbyterian Church of Skaneateles, New York, including the time of the Church's Business Administrator and Pastor. All of the financial records were professionally audited, annually, in order to guarantee professionalism and propriety. All of the Board of Directors of the Foundation are unpaid volunteers, who give their time, personal contacts and expertise to make a difference. By using part-time staff, college students, and volunteers, while operating a "virtual office," JDF has been a model of organizational efficiency, remaining focused on its core mission of providing healthcare in a place where no such services previously existed.

According to a 2010 survey sponsored by the United Nation's Development Programme's Emergency Response Fund, the prevalence of Acute Malnutrition was particularly high in Duk Payuel, where Global Acute Malnutrition rate (GAM) of 20.2% and Severe Acute Malnutrition (SAM) of 6.1% were recorded, compared to WHO World Health Organization) Threshold Limits of 15.0% and 4.0% respectively. The very poor and poor, who comprise 60-75% of the population, are particularly affected and hard-pressed. But the Clinic has produced tangible improvements: according to the same survey, the Crude Mortality Rate (CMR) of 0.83 deaths/10,000/day and Under 5-year-old Mortality Rates (U5MR) of 0.61 deaths/10,000/day are below the alert and emergency threshold levels, and 1.6 times lower than figures recorded in a 2004 ACF survey of the area.

The vision and hard work of one of the "Lost Boys" of South Sudan, combined with the dedication of a team of volunteers and professionals who've simply wanted to improve the lives of disadvantaged and vulnerable people in an area so much in need, have created one of South Sudan's best medical facilities. The Duk Lost Boys Clinic is an example of what the future can be for South Sudan, and the extraordinary work that ordinary people can do by giving of themselves to alleviate human suffering.

In January 2014, the Government of South Sudan was split by Tribal Conflict, which then spread across the Nation. The Clinic at Duk Payuel was abandoned as a War-zone. However, this forced JDF to a tipping-point, by suing the Medical Staff now spread across the County at Refugee Camps and Cattle Camps to create multiple Primary Health Care Urgent-care Units. In 2016, as we reclaimed the main Clinic building and replaced equipment, we did so with support of three satellite clinics, and $2,000,000 funding for malnutrition services.

THE CHURCH'S ENDOWMENTS

The church started out with considerable financial strength, as evidenced by the amount of money raised for construction of the first house of worship. It has always been the character of this congregation to be prompt and forehanded in money matters. If the finances fell into arrears from a shortage in the regular sources of income, as they often have, means were always taken in due time to remedy the deficiency. There have been those whose interests have led them to become permanent supporters of the church. In the 1800s, Mrs. Fanny Jewett and Mr. Thomas Hall each gave $1,000 as Endowments, the interest of which to be used for current expenses. Mrs. Fanny Jewett gave another $1,000and Miss Louisa Weller $500 and Mr. Alfred Hitchcock $100, the interest of which to be used for funding the Sunday School and church program.

AN INVESTMENT MINISTRY

In 1919 the church began "A Ministry of Investment." local banks were paying an average of 2% on investments, while Liberty Bonds were invested at 3.5% - 4%. On the other-hand, Mortgages from lending institutions charged home-owners 6 – 7%. The church attempted to protect our own home-owners facing economic hardship while also investing the church's assets at a higher rate of return than otherwise available, by the church providing first mortgages at 5.0 – 5.5% interest. In 1919 $26,650 of the church's assets were invested in Real Estate in and around Skaneateles. By 1925 the church held first mortgages on Real Estate in Skaneateles, Marcellus, and the City of Syracuse, as well as on farms in the townships of Skaneateles, Marcellus, Spafford and Tully. According to the 1938 Annual Financial Report, the church held first mortgages on $70,000 of property, more than half of which was in the City of Syracuse. By the mid-1970s the church learned the difficult lesson of closing financial relationships with people you know and care about, as many of these mortgages were defaulted upon. Soon thereafter, the church began investing assets with a professional brokerage agency. More recently, these assets were moved from the management of a member of the church, in his firm's brokerage, to paying a non-profit professional investment company to manage these funds for the church.

In 2010, Fred Fundis and his wife, left the church an estate of $306,000, on condition that the principal would be re-invested, and the interest/income was available to the Session as needed annually. In 2013, the Session created a Wills Emphasis program, encouraging members to remember the Church in their Will, by making a pledge of their Estate. This simple recommendation generated a great response from the congregation.

PRESBYTERIAN MANOR

In 1972, church member Don Dixon thought it a shame that persons who had lived their entire lives in this community often had to move into Nursing Homes when they were still healthy and relatively independent. Mr. Dixon set about purchasing and operating a Boarding House for Seniors, which for "The Well Elderly" provided all meals and utilities and a private room for an affordable fixed cost. After opening "Presbyterian Manor" Mr. Dixon began gifting this mission to the church over a period of several years. Mr. Dixon added to the provision of his Will that should the church not maintain the operation of Presbyterian Manor for 10 years, that the proceeds would be sold and the cash given to another mission cause. However, the First Presbyterian Church has continued this mission from 1972 until the present, providing a lovely home for those not ready to consider or need nursing care. In 1998, the Session committed to a re-building of Presbyterian Manor, converting private rooms into suites, each of which have a bed room, a sitting room and their own private full bath. In addition, in recent years, the church has installed new furnaces, new windows, new siding, new roof, new porches, new kitchen, air conditioning, new carpeting and papering throughout.

A DIIFERENT WAY OF FUNDING MISSION

First Presbyterian Church has always been generous in funding missions. For several decades throughout the 1800s, this congregation contributed $600 - $800 per year to The Freedmen Fund in order to purchase the freedom of one human slave per year. Support of the Freedmen, Home Missions and Foreign Missions, Auburn Theological Seminary, The Temperance Society and other charitable works accounted for $800 annually. In those years, the total budget of the church was $2,470. By 1950 the amount given to missions had increased to $4,618 and by 1963 benevolences were $8,700 while by the year 2000, in addition to providing Presbyterian Manor, the church was contributing $98,000 year to Mission causes a full 31% of the Operating Giving. About this time, it was discovered that in earlier times, the funding of missions was through special offerings in addition to the operating budget of the church. The Freedmen's Offering was received on the 3rd Sabbath in February. The Synodical Sustentation Fund to assist "feeble churches in NY State had an offering on the 3rd Sabbath in March and July. Aid for Colleges was received on the 3rd Sabbath in April. The Temperance Fund for the Support of Women, under the direction of the General Assembly of the Presbyterian Church was received on the 3rd Sabbath in May. The Offering for Ministerial Relief was received the 3rd Sundays in June and November, assisting the families of ministers in cases of disability or death. An offering for Christian Education, for Church Erection, for the Deacons, and for Ladies Aid Society, were also received.

It was determined that in addition to the Session funding Presbyterian Mission Causes and local Mission Causes through the Operating Budget, that the church could create as separate non-profit 501c3 corporations various mission causes, which the church would like to see extending the work of the church, while no longer under control of the church. Presbyterian Manor annually received and spent in excess of $120,000. The Sudanese Clinic began at $350,000 per year and grew to a budget of in excess of $500,000 annually. The Skaneateles Festival while not a mission of the church used the church Sanctuary free of charge for the entire month of August each year to provide classical chamber music to the populace. In total, all of the various different groups created by and responsible to First Presbyterian Church raised and spent in excess of $2,250,000 annually, while the church maintained an operating budget of $350,000 with 10% of that going to missions. No longer did the church have control of the activities of these charitable organizations, but they were carrying out the kind of work the church would have wanted to provide, while being funded outside the church.

CONCLUSION

We must end as we began, with the words of Rev. O.L. White, ...

"This has not by any means been an ideal church, the perfect church is in heaven. Another history may have been written, whose tone would be adversely critical, in which the facts stated would be justifiably censurable because of folly or maliciousness. But every historian or biographer omits more than (s)he records, and wisely. Among the early settlers were men of military title, and they carried their belligerent propensities into church matters as well. Considering the number of such experiences, it is a wonder that the church ever survived. Bitter feelings engendered, and autocratic inquisitorial exercise of power, resulted in several divisions within this body. It is no small thing, to have been an organization, in which a thousand souls (or 3,000) have confessed their faith in Jesus Christ, and acknowledged his mastery, while half as many more having come from other churches have cast their lot in and found a religious home. We believe in God; we believe in his purpose for us in the future, and therefore we have abundant courage. We begin the second Century (now our third) under auspicious skies. Undoubtedly there will be dark periods; there have been many in the century(ies) past; hardships and sacrifices, doubtless will be required – they have been before – but with a mighty God, with faithful, loyal members, with a universal gospel invitation to proclaim, with daily grace from the God of all graces, and the covenant that as our days our strength shall be, we resolutely face the future, actuated by Christian faith, hope and courage."

As described by Reinhold Niebuhr, the Church is continually struggling with its identity as part of, and yet apart from the Culture, recognizing that we have the same citizens, and are effected by the same influences. There have been times, when mores in the society and within the church were challenged. There have been eras when the church reacted defensively, avoiding and postponing major repairs as too costly, rather than boldly acting upon dreams. There have also been times when the church led the culture by taking risks others would not consider possible, and attempting to redeem persons who were lost. May future historians treat us with grace and kindness as the church continues to act in mission and service.

www.ingramcontent.com/pod-product-compliance
Lightning Source LLC
Chambersburg PA
CBHW071530080526
44588CB00011B/1617